Flowers in CROSS STITCH

Jane Alford•Dorothea Hall•Shirley Watts

CONTENTS

*I*NTRODUCTION

From the early days of samplers, when small girls were made to practise their embroidery skills until they reached perfection, flowers have been a cherished and favoured theme, their delicate beauty being ideally suited to interpretation in embroidery threads and fine stitchery. Today, when so much of the countryside is threatened with the advent of herbicides and intensive farming methods, and when so many of us live in cities, we can perhaps appreciate the beauty of floral embroideries as never before.

The projects in this book represent a celebration in cross stitch of flowers – including the cultivated beauty of roses, as well as the more fragile loveliness of wild flowers. The designs vary in difficulty from the very simple to the more elaborate. Cross stitch is not only one of the oldest stitches, it is also one of the simplest, and with the help of the instructions on the following pages, even complete beginners will find that many of these designs are well within their scope.

The patterns have been worked on various materials, ranging from perforated paper to fabrics with between 14 and 28 threads per 2.5cm (1in). More experienced cross stitchers may like to experiment by working the designs on different counts to those suggested, perhaps to suit their eyesight. In this case, it is important that you calculate the size of your complete design before you begin.

For those who are new to cross stitch, there are simple designs in the Quick and Easy Gifts section to choose from, as well as several sets of greetings cards, any of which could be framed as a picture. As you gain confidence, you might like to try the larger projects such as the baskets and wreaths cushions. Some of the more advanced projects, such as the panel of wayside flowers or the botanical sampler, use a wide range of colours for shaded effects, and will challenge the more experienced embroiderers.

Whatever your level of skill, you will surely find a project in these pages to catch your eye, and bring a special touch of elegance to your home. Happy stitching!

#

BEFORE YOU BEGIN

PREPARING THE FABRIC

Even with an average amount of handling, many evenweave fabrics tend to fray at the edges, so it is a good idea to overcast the raw edges, using ordinary sewing thread, before you begin.

THE INSTRUCTIONS

Each project begins with a full list of the materials that you will require. All the designs are worked on fabrics such as Aida or Lugana, produced by Zweigart. The measurements given for the embroidery fabric include a minimum of 5cm (2in) all around, to allow for stretching it in a frame and preparing the edges to prevent them from fraying.

Colour keys for stranded embroidery cottons – DMC, Anchor or Maderia – are given with each chart. It is assumed that you will need to buy one skein of each colour mentioned in a particular key even though you may use less, but where two or more skeins are needed, this information is included in the main list of requirements.

To work from the charts, particularly those where several symbols are used in close proximity, some readers may find it helpful to have the chart enlarged so that the squares and symbols can be seen more easily. Many photocopying services will do this.

Before you begin to embroider, always mark the centre of the design with two lines of basting stitches, one vertical and one horizontal, running from edge to edge of the fabric, as indicated by the arrows on the charts.

As you stitch, use the centre lines given on the chart and the basting threads on your fabric as reference points for counting the squares and threads to position your design accurately.

WORKING IN A HOOP

A hoop is the most popular frame for use with small areas of embroidery. It consists of two rings, one fitted inside the other; the outer ring usually has an adjustable screw attachment so that it can be tightened to hold the stretched fabric in place. Hoops are available in several sizes, ranging from 10cm (4in) in diameter to quilting hoops with a diameter of 38cm (15in). Hoops with table stands or floor stands attached are also available.

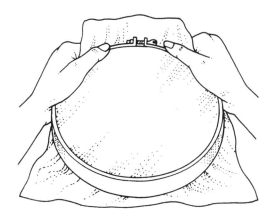

1 To stretch your fabric in a hoop, place the area to be embroidered over the inner ring and press the outer ring over it, with the tension screw released. Tissue paper can be placed between the outer ring and the embroidery, so that the hoop does not mark the fabric. Lay the tissue paper over the fabric when you set it in the hoop, then tear away the central embroidery area.

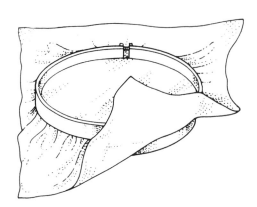

2 Smooth the fabric and, if necessary, straighten the grain before tightening the screw. The fabric should be evenly stretched.

EXTENDING EMBROIDERY FABRIC

It is easy to extend a piece of embroidery fabric, such as a bookmark, to stretch it in a hoop.

● Fabric oddments of a similar weight can be used. Simply cut four pieces to size (in other words, to the measurement that will fit both the embroidery fabric and your hoop) and baste them to each side of the embroidery fabric before stretching it in the hoop in the usual way.

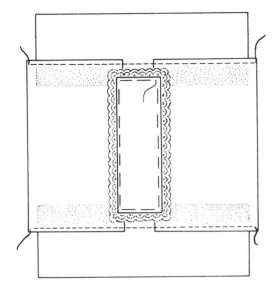

WORKING IN A RECTANGULAR FRAME

Rectangular frames are more suitable for larger pieces of embroidery. They consist of two rollers, with tapes attached, and two flat side pieces, which slot into the rollers and are held in place by pegs or screw attachments. Available in different sizes, either alone or with adjustable table or floor stands, frames are measured by the length of the roller tape, and range in size from 30cm (12in) to 68cm (27in).

As alternatives to a slate frame, canvas stretchers and the backs of old picture frames can be used. Provided there is sufficient extra fabric around the finished size of the embroidery, the edges can be turned under and simply attached with drawing pins (thumb tacks) or staples.

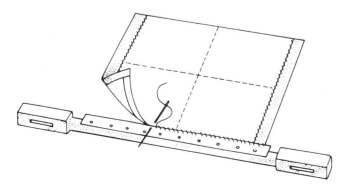

1 To stretch your fabric in a rectangular frame, cut out the fabric, allowing at least an extra 5cm (2in)

all around the finished size of the embroidery. Baste a single 12mm (½in) turning on the top and bottom edges and oversew strong tape, 2.5cm (1in) wide, to the other two sides. Mark the centre line both ways with basting stitches. Working from the centre outward and using strong thread, oversew the top and bottom edges to the roller tapes. Fit the side pieces into the slots, and roll any extra fabric on one roller until the fabric is taut.

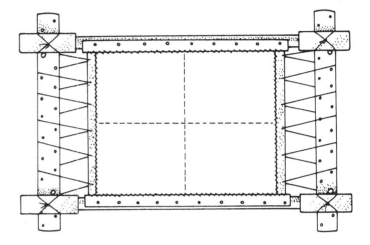

2 Insert the pegs or adjust the screw attachments to secure the frame. Thread a large-eyed needle (chenille needle) with strong thread or fine string and lace both edges, securing the ends around the intersections of the frame. Lace the webbing at 2.5cm (1in) intervals, stretching the fabric evenly.

TO MITRE A CORNER

Press a single hem to the wrong side, the same as the measurement given in the instructions. Open the hem out again and fold the corner of the fabric inwards as shown on the diagram. Refold the hem to the wrong side along the pressed line, and slip-stitch in place.

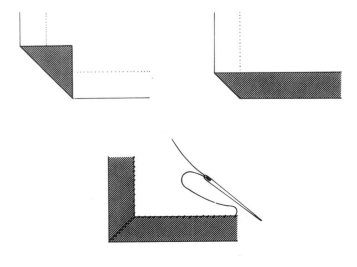

MOUNTING EMBROIDERY

The cardboard should be cut to the size of the finished embroidery, with an extra 6mm (½in) added all round to allow for the recess in the frame.

LIGHTWEIGHT FABRICS

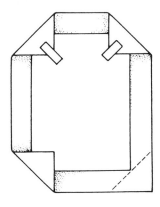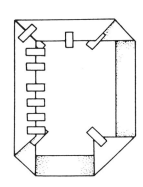

1 Place embroidery face down, with the cardboard centred on top, and basting and pencil lines matching. Begin by folding over the fabric at each corner and securing it with masking tape.

2 Working first on one side and then the other, fold over the fabric on all sides and secure it firmly with pieces of masking tape, placed about 2.5cm (1in) apart. Also neaten the mitred corners with masking tape, pulling the fabric tightly to give a firm, smooth finish.

HEAVIER FABRICS

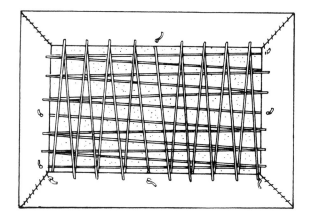

● Lay the embroidery face down, with the cardboard centred on top; fold over the edges of the fabric on opposite sides, making mitred folds at the corners, and lace across, using strong thread. Repeat on the other two sides. Finally, pull up the fabric firmly over the cardboard. Overstitch the mitred corners.

PIPED SEAMS

Contrasting piping adds a special decorative finish to a seam and looks particularly attractive on items such as cushions and cosies.

You can cover piping cord with either bias-cut fabric of your choice or a bias binding: alternatively, ready covered piping cord is available in several widths and many colours.

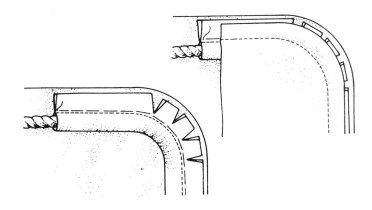

1 To apply piping, pin and baste it to the right side of the fabric, with seam lines matching. Clip into the seam allowance where necessary.

2 With right sides together, place the second piece of fabric on top, enclosing the piping. Baste and then either hand stitch in place or machine stitch, using a zipper foot. Stitch as close to the piping as possible, covering the first line of stitching.

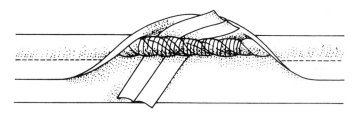

3 To join ends of piping cord together, first overlap the two ends by about 2.5cm (1in). Unpick the two cut ends of bias to reveal the cord. Join the bias strip as shown. Trim and press the seam open. Unravel and slice the two ends of the cord. Fold the bias strip over it, and finish basting around the edge.

TO BIND AN EDGE

1 Open out the turning on one edge of the bias binding and pin in position on the right side of the fabric, matching the fold to the seamline. Fold over the cut end of the binding. Finish by overlapping the starting point by about 12mm (½in). Baste and machine stitch along the seam.

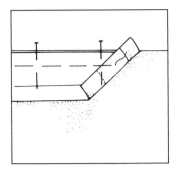 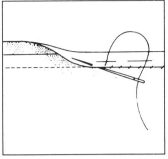

2 Fold the binding over the raw edge to the worng side, baste and, using matching sewing thread, neatly hem to finish.

CROSS STITCH

For all cross stitch embroidery, the following two methods of working are used. In each case, neat rows of vertical stitches are produced on the back of the fabric.

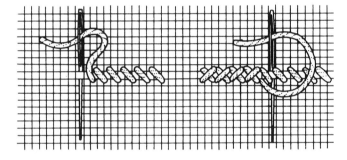

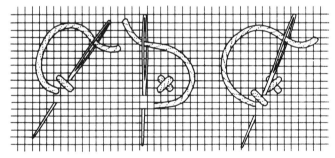

● When stitching large areas, work in horizontal rows. Working from right to left, complete the first row of evenly spaced diagonal stitches over the number of threads specified in the project instructions. Then, working from left to right, repeat the process. Continue in this way, making sure each stitch crosses in the same direction.

● When stitching diagonal lines, work downwards, completing each stitch before moving to the next. When starting a project always begin to embroider at the centre of the design and work outwards to ensure that the design will be placed centrally on the fabric.

FRENCH KNOTS

This stitch is shown on some of the diagrams by a small dot. Where there are several french knots, the dots have been omitted to avoid confusion. Where this occurs you should refer to the instructions of the project and the colour photograph.

To work a french knot, bring your needle and cotton out slightly to the right of where you want your knot to be. Wind the thread once or twice around the needle, depending on how big you want your knot to be, and insert the needle to the left of the point where you brought it out.

Be careful not to pull too hard or the knot will disappear through the fabric. The instructions state the number of strands of cotton to be used for the french knots.

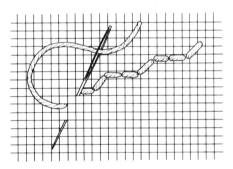

BACKSTITCH

Backstitch is used in the projects to give emphasis to a particular foldline, an outline or a shadow. The stitches are worked over the same number of threads as the cross stitch, forming continuous straight or diagonal lines.

● Make the first stitch from left to right; pass the needle behind the fabric and bring it out one stitch length ahead to the left. Repeat and continue in this way along the line.

ADDING NAMES AND DATES

First of all, on a spare piece of graph paper, draw your names and dates, using the alphabet given for that particular project. Count the number of stitches in the width of each name or date and mark the centre. When you have done this draw the names and dates again, matching the centres with the centre of the sampler.

SPECIAL OCCASIONS AND CELEBRATIONS

Birthdays, weddings, the arrival of a new member of the family, moving to a new home — embroiderers celebrate these landmarks with a decorative picture to be treasured.
This section includes lovely samplers, including some that are traditional and others, such as the stork sampler, that are more modern. There are also greetings cards for family and friends, plus some enchanting keepsake designs for a bride and attendants.

Wild Flower Cards

Delicate wild flowers have been used to create a charming trio of cards, which could be used for best wishes or congratulations.

WILD FLOWER CARDS

YOU WILL NEED

For the Red Campion card, measuring
20.5cm × 15cm (8in × 6in), with a rectangular
portrait cut-out measuring 14cm × 9cm
(5½in × 3½in):

*18cm × 14cm (7¼in × 5½in) of cream, 18-count
Aida fabric*
*18cm × 14cm (7¼in × 5½in) of iron-on
interfacing*
*Stranded embroidery cotton in the colours given
in the appropriate panel*
No26 tapestry needle
Greetings card blank (for suppliers, see page 160)

For the Bluebell card, measuring 20.5cm × 15cm
(8in × 6in), with an oval cut-out measuring
14cm × 9cm (5½in × 3½in):

*18cm × 14cm (7¼in × 5½in) of cream, 18-count
Aida fabric*
*18cm × 14cm (7¼in × 5½in) of iron-on
interfacing*
*Stranded embroidery cotton in the colours given
in the appropriate panel*
No26 tapestry needle
Greetings card blank (for suppliers, see page 160)

For the Wild Pansy card, measuring 12cm × 9cm
(4¾in × 3½in), with an oval cut-out measuring
8.5cm × 6.5cm (3¼in × 2½in):

*13.5cm × 9cm (5¼in × 3½in) of cream,
18-count Aida fabric*
*13.5cm × 9cm (5¼in × 3½in) of iron-on
interfacing*
*Stranded embroidery cotton in the colours given
in the appropriate panel*
No26 tapestry needle
Greetings card blank (for suppliers, see page 160)

•

THE EMBROIDERY

All three cards are stitched in the same way and
on the same type of fabric.

Note that it is particularly important with
embroidered cards to avoid excessive overstitching

on the back, as this would cause unsightly lumps
to show through on the right side.

Prepare the fabric, marking the centre lines of
each design with basting stitches, and mount it
in a hoop, following the instructions on page 8.
Referring to the appropriate chart, complete the
cross stitching, using two strands in the needle
throughout. Embroider the main areas first, and
then finish with the backstitching. If necessary,
steam press on the wrong side.

MAKING UP THE CARDS

Iron the interfacing to the back of the embroidery,
and trim both to about 12mm (½in) larger all around
than the cut-out window. This will help to prevent
the mounted picture from wrinkling. Position the
embroidery behind the window.

Open out the self-adhesive mount and centre your
embroidery behind the aperture. Fold the card and
press firmly to secure. Some cards require a dab of
glue to ensure a secure and neat finish.

WILD PANSY ▼		DMC	ANCHOR	MADEIRA
	White*	White	2	White
—	Light mauve	554	97	0711
⌐	Medium mauve	552	101	0713
x	Dark mauve	550	102	0714
·	Yellow	726	295	0109
+	Dark green	3346	817	1407
■	Black	310	403	Black

Note: outline flower centres in white*.

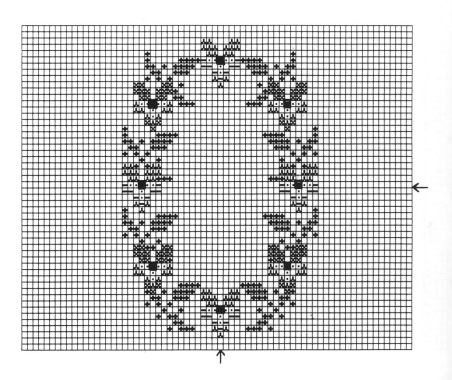

RED CAMPION ▼	DMC	ANCHOR	MADEIRA
I Pale pink	3609	85	0710
∴ Pink	3608	86	0709
T Deep pink	3607	87	0708
U Purplish red	315	896	0810
— Pale green	3348	264	1409
ï Green	3347	266	1408
+ Dark green	3346	817	1407

Note: bks flower stems and centres in green.

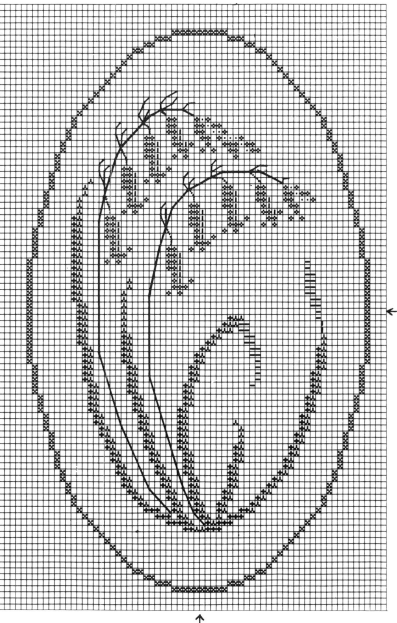

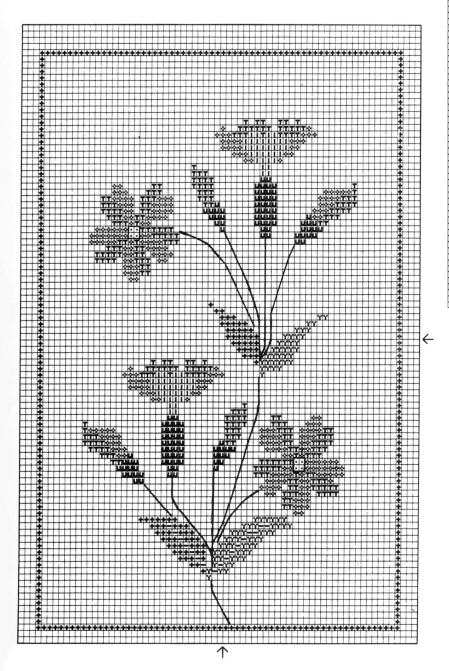

BLUEBELL ▲	DMC	ANCHOR	MADEIRA
· Light mauve	210	108	0802
I Pale blue	341	117	0901
∴ Blue	340	118	0902
x Light navy	792	177	0905
— Light green	3347	266	1408
⅃ Medium green	3346	817	1407
+ Dark green	3345	268	1406

Note: bks flowers stalks in light mauve, bracts in pale blue, leaf blade in dark green, and main stems in light green.

Wedding Sampler

A wedding is a great family occasion,
so why not add your congratulations
in cross stitch with a beautiful
wedding sampler? Stitched on white
evenweave linen, the shades of pink,
peach and blue are perfect for the
profusion of flowers and ribbons
that make up the border.
The hearts surrounding the names are
a reminder of the love and affection
the couple share.

WEDDING SAMPLER

Instructions for using an alphabet to write your own name and date are at the beginning of the book.

YOU WILL NEED

For the Wedding Bells sampler, with a design area measuring 24cm × 25cm (9½in × 10in), or 124 stitches by 129 stitches, here in a frame measuring 36cm × 38cm (14½in × 15¼in):

34cm × 35cm (13½in × 14in) of white, 25-count Lugana fabric
Stranded embroidery cotton in the colours given in the panel
No24 tapestry needle
Strong thread, for lacing across the back
Cardboard for mounting, sufficient to fit into the frame recess
Frame of your choice

●

THE EMBROIDERY

Prepare the fabric and stretch it in a frame as explained on page 9. Following the chart, start the embroidery at the centre of the design, using two strands of embroidery cotton in the needle. Work each stitch over two threads of fabric in each direction. Make sure that all the top crosses run in the same direction and that each row is worked into the same holes as the top or bottom of the row before, so that you do not leave a space between the rows.

With backstitch and using one strand of dark grey cotton, outline the bells and flowers, then embroider the date, month and year with two strands of dark grey cotton. The flower stalks are worked with two strands of medium green cotton in backstitch. Instructions for using an alphabet to write your own name and date are at the beginning of the book.

Work the centres of the blue flowers with french knots in light peach cotton.

MAKING UP

Gently steam press the work on the wrong side and mount it as explained on page 10. Choose an appropriate frame and mount to add the final touch to this record of a very special day.

WEDDING SAMPLER ▶		DMC	ANCHOR	MADEIRA
▪	Light pink	3689	66	0606
⊞	Dark pink	3688	68	0605
⊟	Light mauve	211	108	0801
⊠	Dark mauve	210	109	0803
✳	Light peach	353	9	0304
◹	Dark peach	758	9575	0403
❘	Light blue	800	128	0908
◉	Medium blue	799	130	0910
▲	Dark blue	798	131	0911
⊓	Light green	3348	264	1409
⊠	Medium green	3052	844	1509
▲	Dark green	936	263	1507
◇	Light grey	415	398	1803
◼	Dark grey	414	399	1801

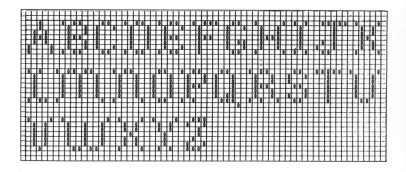

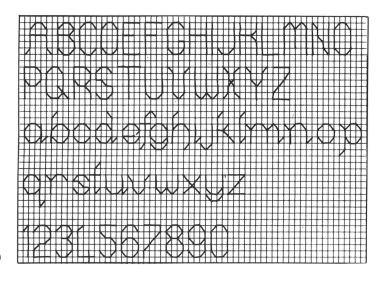

Floral Feast

A selection of traditional flower motifs have been arranged to create an attractive floral sampler, which could be made to celebrate a birth, a wedding or any other major family event. The pinks in the basket of roses are echoed in the daisy-like flowers at the top of the sampler and complement the mauve shades of the other flowers.

FLORAL FEAST

For the Floral Feast sampler, with a design area measuring 18.5cm × 21cm (7½in × 8¼in), or 101 stitches by 119 stitches, here in a frame measuring 31cm × 35cm (12¼in × 14in):

28.5cm × 31cm (11½in × 12¼in) of white, 14-count Aida fabric
Stranded embroidery cotton in the colours given in the panel
No24 tapestry needle
Strong thread, for lacing across the back
Cardboard, for mounting, sufficient to fit into the frame recess
Frame of your choice

•

THE EMBROIDERY

Prepare the fabric and stretch it in a frame as explained on page 9. Following the chart, start the embroidery at the centre of the design, using two strands of embroidery cotton in the needle. Work each stitch over one block of fabric in each direction. Make sure that all the top crosses run in the same direction and each row is worked into the same holes as the top or bottom of the row before so that you do not leave a space between the rows.

Embroider your name and the date, following the instructions on page 11. The basket of flowers has here been framed as a picture, but it could also be used as a design for a small pincushion.

MAKING UP

Gently steam press the work on the wrong side and mount it as explained on page 10. As this is a sampler with traditional motifs, it has been framed without a mount so that it is in keeping with the samplers stitched around the turn of the century. The rose motif would look most attractive as a separate picture, and other motifs could also be extracted and used in this manner, perhaps with minor modifications.

FLORAL FEAST ▶		DMC	ANCHOR	MADEIRA
‹	Light pink	604	60	0614
+	Medium pink	603	63	0701
o	Dark pink	600	65	0704
%	Light mauve	210	108	0803
–	Dark mauve	208	111	0804
v	Yellow	743	301	0113
s	Light green	369	213	1309
=	Medium green	320	215	1311
‡	Dark green	367	217	1312
X	Light brown	729	890	2209
›	Dark brown	434	365	2009

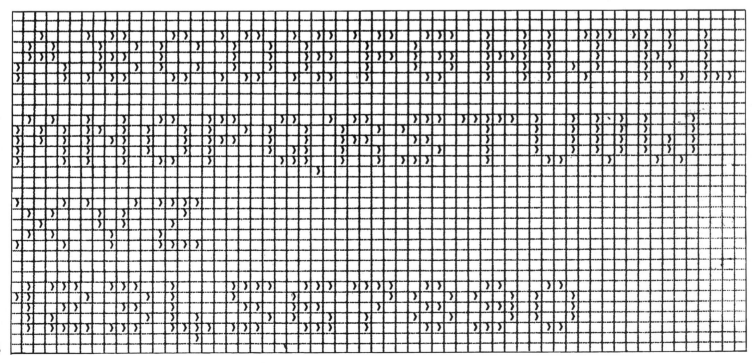

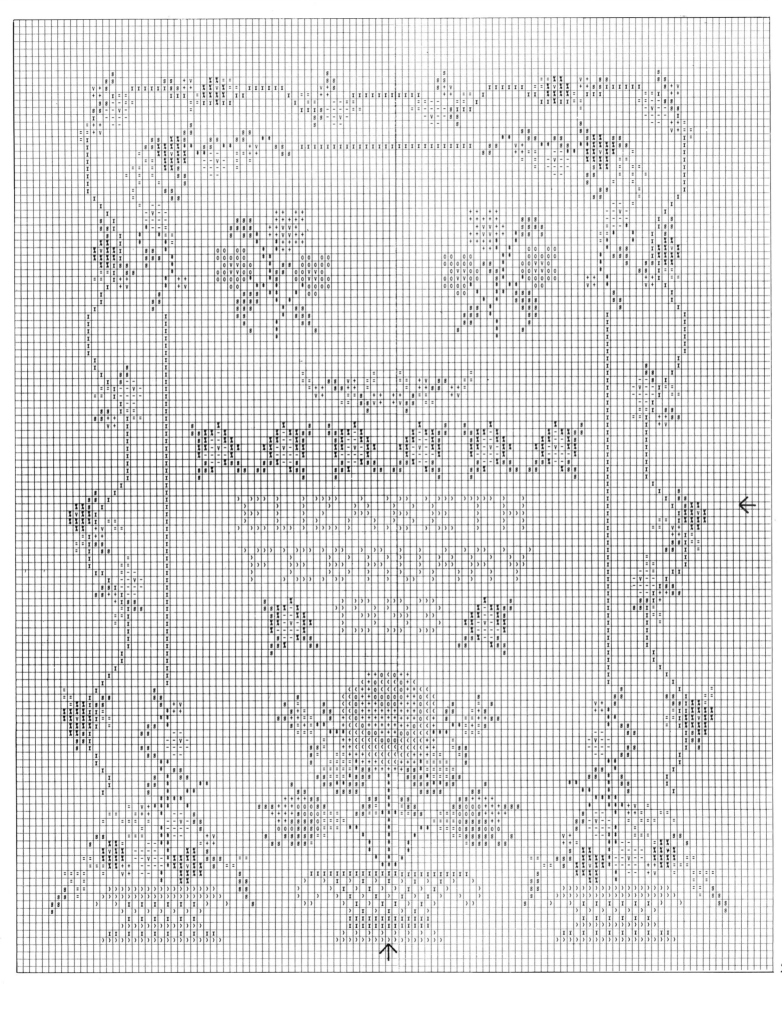

Say it with Roses

Whichever of these attractive greetings cards you embroider, the result will provide a lasting reminder of a special occasion, as the finished card can easily be framed.

SAY IT WITH ROSES

YOU WILL NEED

For either the Rosy Posy card or the Wild Rose card, each measuring 15cm × 20.5cm (6in × 8in) overall, with a portrait cut-out measuring 11cm × 15cm (4½in × 6in):

15cm × 19cm (6in × 7½in) of cream, 18-count Aida fabric
Stranded embroidery cotton in the colours given in the appropriate panel
No24 tapestry needle
Card mount, landscape or portrait, as required (for suppliers, see page 160)

For the Rose Garland card, measuring 15.5cm × 11cm (6¼in × 4½in), with a cut-out measuring 8cm (3in) in diameter:

10cm (4in) square of cream, 18-count Aida fabric
Stranded embroidery cotton in the colours given in the appropriate panel
No24 tapestry needle
Card mount (for suppliers, see page 160)

•

THE EMBROIDERY

Prepare the fabric for your chosen card and stretch it in a frame as explained on page 9. Following the appropriate chart, start the embroidery at the centre of the design, using one strand of embroidery cotton in the needle. Work each stitch over one block of fabric in each direction. Make sure that all the top crosses go in the same direction and that each row is worked into the same holes as the top or bottom of the row before, so that you do not leave a space between the rows.

MAKING UP THE CARDS

Trim the embroidery to about 12mm (½in) larger than the cut-out window. Open out the self-adhesive mount and centre your embroidery behind the aperture. Fold the card and press firmly to secure. Some cards require a dab of glue for a secure and neat finish.

WILD ROSE ▶		DMC	ANCHOR	MADEIRA
⊡	Light pink	818	48	0502
△	Medium pink	776	73	0606
⊟	Dark pink	899	40	0609
⊞	Light yellow	3078	292	0102
⊞	Medium yellow	743	301	0113
⊟	Light green	3348	264	1409
⊞	Medium green	3347	266	1408
◆	Dark green	3345	268	1406
⊡	Light brown	434	365	2009
●	Medium brown	829	906	2106

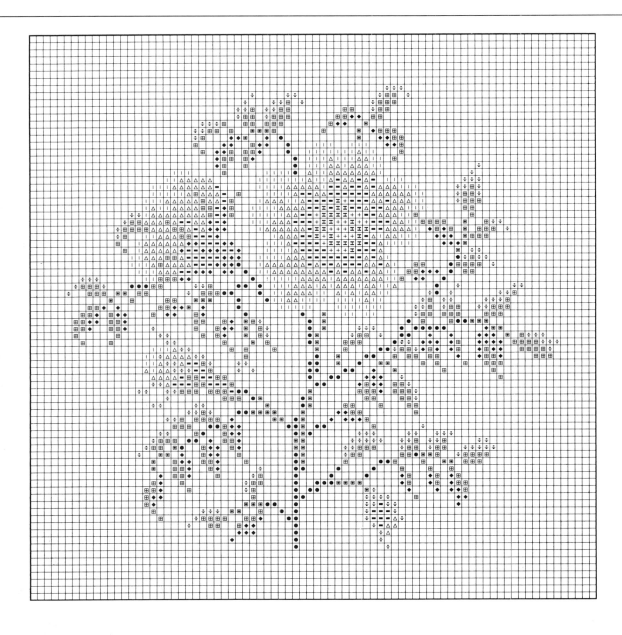

ROSY POSY ◄		DMC	ANCHOR	MADEIRA
⊟	Light pink	894	26	0408
⋀	Medium pink	892	28	0413
⊞	Dark pink	304	47	0511
△	Light green	3348	264	1409
⊡	Medium green	3052	844	1509
♥	Dark green	3051	845	1508

ROSE GARLAND ►		DMC	ANCHOR	MADEIRA
◿	Light pink	776	73	0606
⊵	Medium pink	899	40	0609
▲	Dark pink	309	42	0510
⊥	Light peach	948	778	0306
⊞	Medium peach	353	6	0304
◪	Dark peach	754	868	0305
✕	Yellow	743	301	0113
⊞	Light blue	932	920	1602
▬	Medium blue	931	921	1003
♥	Dark blue	930	922	1005
▷	Light green	3348	264	1409
M	Medium green	470	266	1502
▼	Dark green	936	263	1507

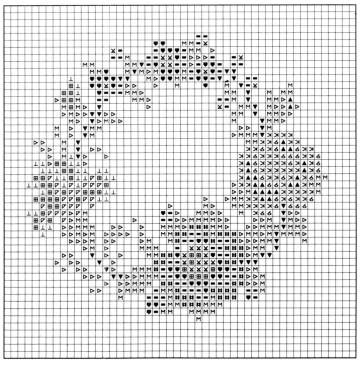

Celebration Cushions

A pretty cushion, embroidered to celebrate a particular occasion, always makes a very acceptable gift. Each motif – confetti-strewn wedding bells, a floral Valentine heart and a Christmas wreath of poinsettias and holly – is bordered with ribbon, bows or braid, and each cushion is finished with delicate lace trim.

CELEBRATION CUSHIONS

YOU WILL NEED

For the Wedding Anniversary cushion, measuring overall 25cm (10in) square:

Two 25cm (10in) squares of white,
18-count Davosa
Stranded embroidery cotton in the colours
given in the appropriate panel
140cm (1½yd) of white lace trim, 2.5cm
(1in) wide
Gold embroidery thread for the border
23cm (9in) square cushion pad
No26 tapestry needle
Matching sewing thread

For the Christmas Time cushion, measuring overall 25cm (10in) square:

Two 25cm (10in) squares of khaki, 16-count Aida
Stranded embroidery cotton in the colours
given in the appropriate panel
140cm (1½yd) of deep cream lace trim, 2cm
(¾in) wide
23cm (9in) square cushion pad
No24 tapestry needle
Matching sewing thread

For the Valentine cushion, measuring overall 25cm (10in) square:

Two 23cm (9in) squares of white, 21-count linen
Stranded embroidery cotton in the colours
given in the appropriate panel
140cm (1½yd) of white lace trim, 4cm
(1½in) wide
180cm (2yd) of pink parcel ribbon
20cm (8in) square cushion pad
No26 tapestry needle
Matching sewing thread

WEDDING ANNIVERSARY

Baste the centre both ways on one of the squares of fabric and stretch it in a hoop, see page 8. Following the chart and colour key, and using two strands of thread in the needle throughout, begin the embroidery, stitching the gold thread details first. On this fabric, it is better to work one complete cross stitch at a time, over each intersection, to prevent the threads from slipping. Finish the embroidery and then outline the base of the bells in silver thread. Steam press on the wrong side.

For the border, follow the chart and, using two strands of gold thread in the needle, embroider the double lines, stitching under one thread and over five. Make sure that the pattern of stitching is the same on each line.

MAKING UP THE CUSHION

Trim the embroidery to measure 21.5cm (8½in) square. Using a tiny french seam, join the short edges of the lace together.

Run a gathering thread close to the straight edge of the lace. Pulling up the gathers to fit, lay the lace on the right side of the embroidery, with the decorative edge facing inwards and the straight edge parallel to the edge of the fabric and just inside the seam allowance. Baste in position, adjusting the gathers to allow extra fullness at the corners. Machine stitch in place.

With the right sides together, centre the backing fabric over the embroidered fabric and lace. Trim to size, then baste and machine stitch around, leaving a 13cm (5in) opening in the middle of one side. Remove all basting stitches; trim across the seam allowance at the corners, and turn the cover right side out. Insert the cushion pad and slipstitch the opening to close it.

CHRISTMAS TIME

Following the appropriate chart, complete the embroidery as for the Wedding Anniversary cushion. In this case, however, the design is embroidered on Aida fabric, so the cross stitches can be made in two stages, if you prefer. Embroider the backstitch details last of all.

Steam press the embroidery on the wrong side. Trim the embroidery and backing fabric 24cm (9½in) square. Add the lace edging and make up the cushion following the previous instructions.

VALENTINE

Stretch the prepared fabric in a hoop and, following the relevant chart, complete the embroidery, using two strands of thread in the needle and working one cross stitch over two threads throughout. Steam press the finished embroidery on the wrong side.

For the ribbon border, cut the parcel ribbon into four 27.5cm (11in) lengths and four 17.5cm (7in) lengths. Withdraw a single thread from the ground fabric on each side, six threads out from the embroidered motif.

Following the diagram, thread one short length of ribbon from a point where two drawn-thread lines intersect and out to the nearest edge; take the ribbon under four threads and over six, leaving a tail for tying at the intersection.

Thread a longer length from the opposite edge of the fabric to meet the first at the same intersection, again leaving a tying thread at this point. Repeat

on all sides to complete the ribbon border. The bows are tied after the cushion seams have been stitched, securing the outer ends of the ribbons.

FINISHING THE CUSHION

Trim the embroidery and the backing fabric to measure 20cm (8in) square. Add the lace edging and complete the cushion, following the instructions for the Wedding Anniversary cushion.

CHRISTMAS TIME ▼		DMC	ANCHOR	MADEIRA
◣	Yellow	725	306	0108
○	Pink	604	51	0504
⊡	Deep pink	600	65	0704
✳	Red	606	335	0209
•	Purple	915	70	0705
◆	Pale yellow	772	264	1604
△	Yellow green	907	255	1410
I	Pale green	955	203	1210
↓	Veridian green	912	209	1212

Note: bks poinsettias in purple, and leaves in veridian green.

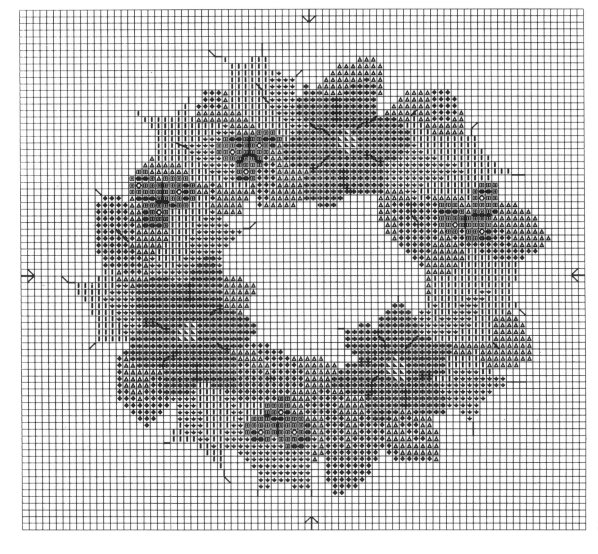

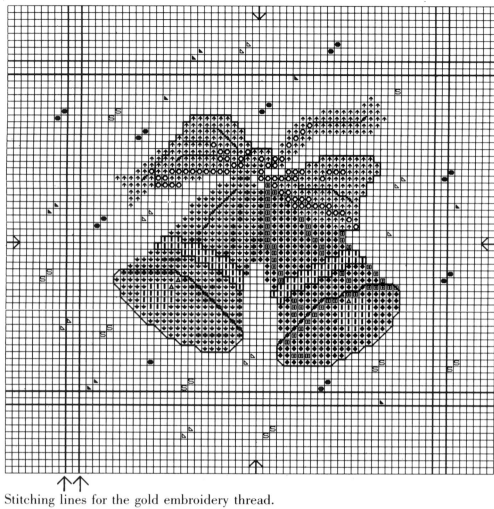

Stitching lines for the gold embroidery thread.

WEDDING ANNIVERSARY ▲		DMC	ANCHOR	MADEIRA
◆	Off white	762	397	1804
△	Silver thread			
↑	Pale yellow	3047	886	2205
O	Yellow	676	891	2209
◺	Rich yellow	725	306	0108
I	Gold thread			
•	Pink	3354	75	0608
S	Pale blue	747	158	1104
◣	Pale green	504	213	1701
⊡	Grey	415	398	1803
↓	Pale green grey	928	900	1709
✱	Green grey	927	849	1708

Note: bks around bell rims in silver thread; make the double border in gold thread; and bks around the off-white bell in grey and the green grey bell in green grey.

VALENTINE ▶		DMC	ANCHOR	MADEIRA
↓	Pink	962	52	0609
•	Red	601	78	0703
O	Bright green	704	256	1308
△	Olive green	733	280	1611
⊡	Dark olive green	732	281	1612
✱	Dark green	520	269	1514

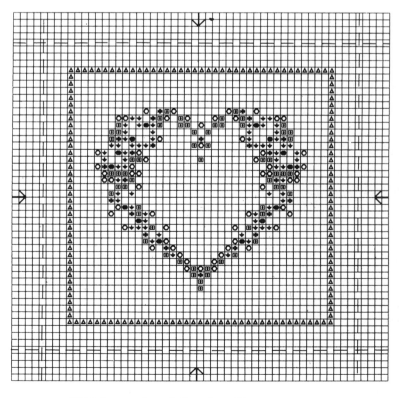

— — — Withdrawn thread line for ribbons.

Lacy Lavender Sachets

Lavender sachets are a traditional idea that will surely never go out of fashion, for sweetly-scented cupboards and drawers are among those finishing touches that are the hallmark of a good hostess. These sachets have been designed to be placed in a drawer, but if you wish to make them for use in wardrobes, you will need to purchase a slightly longer length of ribbon than the amount specified. Although they are called lavender sachets, remember that they can be filled with any type of pot pourri. A summer garden mixture of rose petals would be particularly appropriate for the roses and violets design, for example. Alternatively, the strong, lemony scent of southernwood *(Artemisia abrotanum)* is a traditional defence against moths.

LACY LAVENDER SACHETS

YOU WILL NEED

For one sachet, with an overall measurement of
23cm × 15cm (9in × 6in):

*50cm × 20cm (20in × 8in) of white,
18-count openweave fabric, such as cotton Davosa
or natural linen
32.5cm (13in) of pre-gathered white lace trim,
4cm (1½in) wide
70cm (28in) of double-sided white satin ribbon,
1cm (⅜in) wide
Stranded embroidery cotton in the colours given
in the appropriate panel
No26 tapestry needle
Matching sewing thread
Sufficient lavender or pot pourri to fill the
sachet halfway*

•

THE EMBROIDERY

To transfer the positioning lines to the embroidery,
fold the fabric widthways in half and mark this line
with a pin. Measure 8cm (3in) in from this point
and baste across. Baste the upright centre line.

With the fabric held in a hoop, follow the chart
and complete the motif, using two strands of thread
in the needle. Where several colours are required,
and to save time in starting and finishing, you may
prefer to keep two or three needles in use, pinning
them to the side when those particular colours are
not being used.

Remove the basting stitches and steam press the
finished embroidery on the wrong side.

MAKING UP THE SACHET

With the wrong side facing out, fold the fabric
widthways in half; baste and machine stitch the
sides, taking a 2.5cm (1in) seam. If the edges have
frayed, check that the width of the sachet is 15cm
(6in). Trim the seam allowances to 12mm (½in),
and turn to the right side. Make a 4cm (1½in)
single turning on the top edge and baste.

Join the short edges of the lace trim, using a tiny
french seam. Pin and baste the trim to the inside of the
top edge and, working from the right side, machine
stitch in place, sewing close to the top edge.

Half fill the sachet with lavender and tie the ribbon
twice around the top, finishing with the bow in front.

MARY, MARY ►		DMC	ANCHOR	MADEIRA
‖	White	White	2	White
◇	Pale lemon	745	300	0111
✕	Pale yellow	445	288	0103
◺	Bright yellow	444	291	0108
◆	Deep yellow	783	307	2211
↑	Flesh	948	778	0306
⊡	Pink	605	50	0613
●	Deep pink	603	62	0701
✳	Red	3705	11	0412
=	Pale blue	3761	159	1014
⊖	Turquoise	3766	167	1108
↓	Slate grey	930	922	1712
Ι	Blue	794	120	0907
S	Pale green	564	212	1308
△	Veridian green	958	187	1114
÷	Green	3348	254	1409
◣	Dark green	702	227	1305
○	Khaki	3053	859	1510

*Note: bks butterfly wing and cockle shells with deep yellow, and
bloomers and butterfly body with slate grey.*

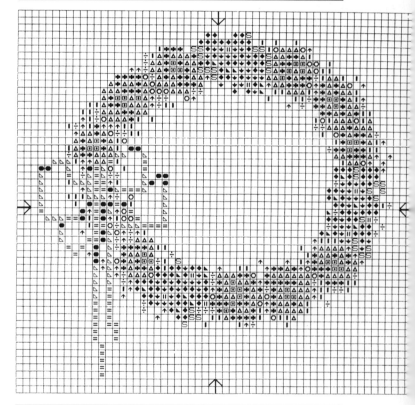

THE ROSE IS RED ▲		DMC	ANCHOR	MADEIRA
‖	Yellow	445	288	0103
△	Pink	3733	75	0505
✳	Magenta	603	62	0701
⊡	Dark red	817	47	0211
◆	Pale blue	341	117	0901
◺	Blue	794	120	0907
●	Deep blue	798	131	0911
◣	Mauve	3609	85	0710
↓	Violet	792	941	0905
=	Turquoise	3761	159	1014
÷	Veridian green	959	186	1113
S	Dark green	943	188	1203
Ι	Green	989	256	1401
↑	Olive	471	280	1501
○	Dark olive	3051	846	1508

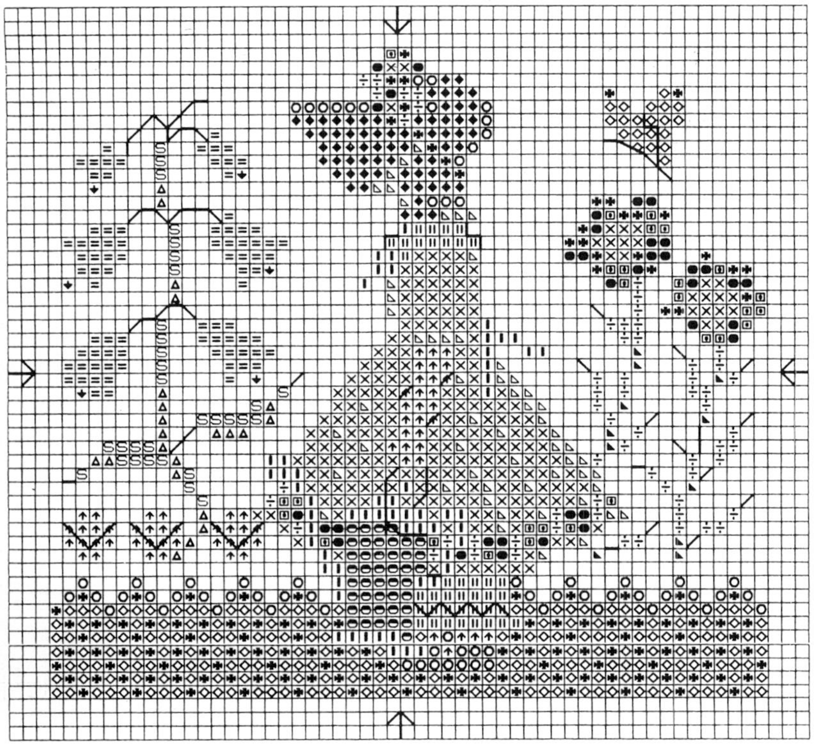

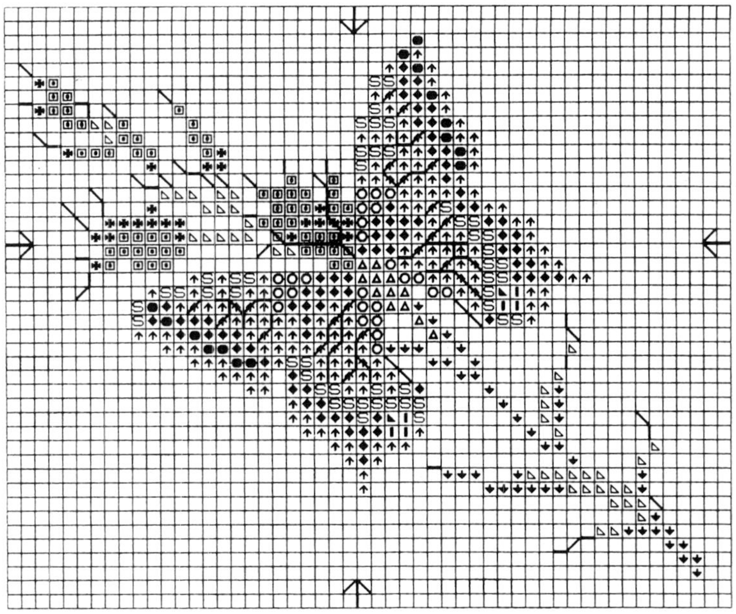

LAVENDER BLUE ▼	DMC	ANCHOR	MADEIRA
✚ Pink	224	893	0813
● Geranium	892	28	0412
⊡ Violet	340	118	0902
△ Blue	341	117	0901
↓ Green	368	261	1310

Note: bks stems in green.

BUTTERFLY ▲	DMC	ANCHOR	MADEIRA
↑ Yellow	445	288	0103
◣ Ochre	783	307	2211
I Orange	721	324	0308
◆ Khaki	734	279	1610
⊡ Pink	602	78	0703
✚ Red	349	13	0212
◺ Green	989	256	1401
↓ Veridian green	993	186	1201
○ Dark green blue	930	922	1712
S Light blue	340	118	0902
● Dark blue	792	941	0905
△ Navy blue	824	164	1010

Note: bks around butterfly wings in khaki.

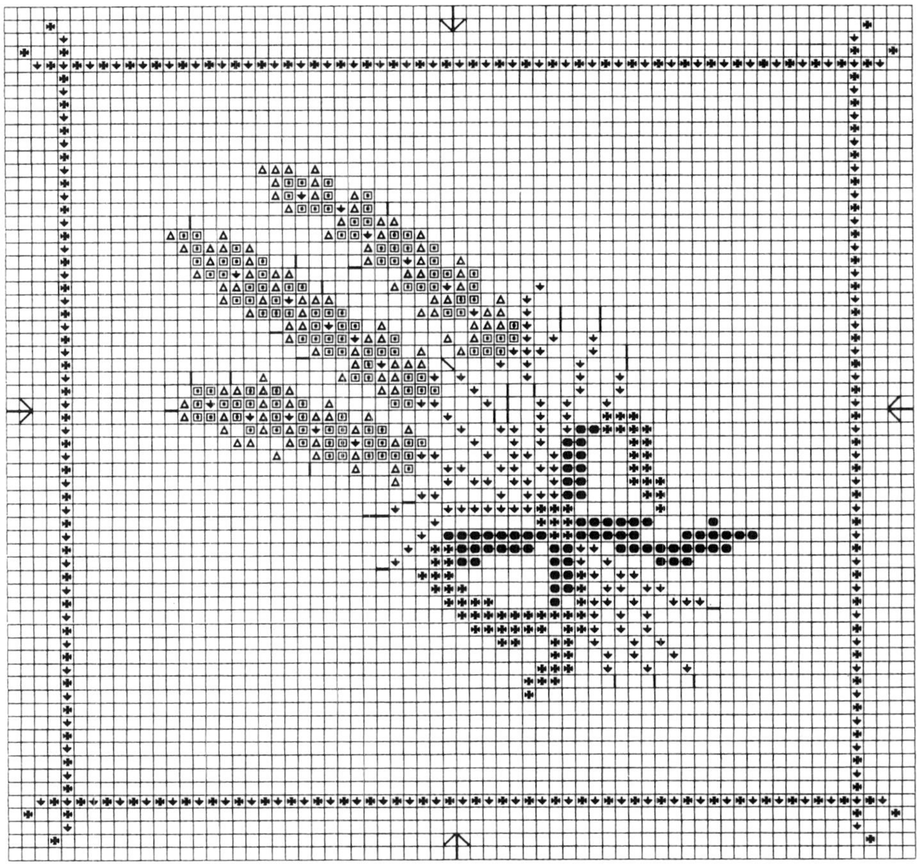

Flowers and Storks Sampler

A new baby! Record the excitement, laughter, joy and celebration in a lovingly-stitched birth sampler. Two slender storks, encircled by a heart, hold a bouquet over the baby's name and date of birth.

The sampler is worked in soft shades of pastel colours to echo those tender feelings a new baby arouses in every heart. The flowers are pink, in the stitched example, but they could easily be changed to blue for a boy.

If the baby has a particularly long name, you could just put the date under the bouquet and add a name panel below the heart, omitting some of the flowers and outlining the panel with dark brown, as for the heart.

FLOWERS AND STORKS SAMPLER

YOU WILL NEED

For the Sampler, with a design area measuring 16cm × 20cm (6¼in × 8in), or 89 stitches by 110 stitches, here in a frame measuring 25cm × 30cm (10in × 12in):

26cm × 30cm (10¼in × 12in) of white, 14-count Aida fabric
Stranded embroidery cotton in the colours given in the panel
No24 tapestry needle
Strong thread, for lacing across the back
Cardboard, for mounting, sufficient to fit into the frame recess
Frame of your choice

•

THE EMBROIDERY

Prepare the fabric and stretch it in a frame (see page 9). Following the chart, start at the centre of the design, using two strands of cotton in the needle. Work each stitch over one block of fabric in each direction. Make sure that all top crosses run in the same direction and that each row is worked into the same holes as the top or bottom of the row before, so that you do not leave a space between rows.

Embroider the leaf stems with two strands of green cotton and the bow with two strands of dark pink cotton. Outline the heart and the storks, and embroider the feet, name and date with one strand of dark brown cotton. If you are making the sampler for a boy, you might choose to embroider the flowers in blue rather than pink.

MAKING UP

Gently steam press the finished embroidery on the wrong side and mount it as explained on page 10. When choosing the mount and frame, consider the colour scheme of the room, as this charming sampler will make a striking and attractive feature.

STORK ▶		DMC	ANCHOR	MADEIRA
+	Cream	746	275	0101
o	Light pink	3689	66	0606
s	Dark pink	3688	68	0605
‡	Green	368	214	1310
‹	Light brown	842	376	1910
=	Dark brown	840	679	1912

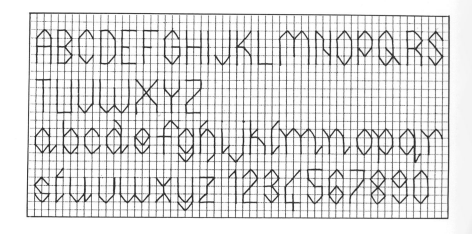

Floral Birthday Cards

Naturalistic flowers and fruits, embroidered on backgrounds of a contrast colour, are featured on this charming trio of birthday cards. Friends and relatives will be delighted to receive them, and cards as pretty as this should be framed after the day and hung as miniatures.

FLORAL BIRTHDAY CARDS

YOU WILL NEED

For the three Birthday greetings cards, each measuring overall 20cm × 14cm (8in × 5½in), with oval portrait cut outs, 14cm × 9.5cm (5½in × 3¾in):

For the *Rose* card:

*23cm × 18cm (9in × 7¼in) of evenweave, 26-count Linda fabric, in pale blue
No26 tapestry needle*

For the *Flower Basket* card:

*23cm × 18cm (9in × 7¼in) of evenweave, 26-count Linda fabric, in yellow
No26 tapestry needle*

For the *Strawberries* card:

*23cm × 18cm (9in × 7¼in) of off white, 20-count linen
No18 tapestry needle*

For each card:

*Stranded embroidery cotton in the colours given in the appropriate panel
Card mount (for suppliers, see page 160)*

•

THE EMBROIDERY

Prepare the fabric (overcasting the edges and basting the centre both ways) and then stretch it in a hoop, see page 8. For all three designs, work one cross stitch over two threads of fabric. For the Flower Basket and Rose designs, embroider with two strands of thread in the No26 needle throughout. For the Strawberries design, use the No18 needle and three strands of thread throughout. Embroider the stems first, and then the strawberries and leaves.

Steam press the finished embroideries on the wrong side. Leave the basting stitches in place at this stage; they will be used later for centring the design in the card.

ASSEMBLING THE CARDS

Open out the self-adhesive card mount; centre your embroidery over the cut-out window (using the basting threads as accurate guide lines), and trim the fabric until it is some 12mm (½in) larger all around than the marked area on the card. Remove the basting stitches. Reposition your embroidery; fold over the left-hand section of the card, and press to secure.

ROSE ▲		DMC	ANCHOR	MADEIRA
∣	Pale yellow	734	279	1610
↓	Yellow	972	303	0107
○	Pale pink	605	50	0613
⊡	Pink	962	52	0609
•	Warm pink	335	42	0506
✹	Magenta	602	78	0703
◆	Green	966	207	1310
△	Veridian green	959	186	1113

Note: bks stems and around leaves in viridian green.

STRAWBERRIES ▼	DMC	ANCHOR	MADEIRA
◆ Pale pink	776	8	0404
↓ Pink	891	35	0411
✱ Red	350	11	0213
• Dark red	817	47	0211
S Green	3348	254	1409
I Sap green	3347	266	1408
O Dark green	937	268	1507
⊡ Ginger	301	370	2306
△ Brown	975	371	2305
◣ Dark brown	3045	888	2103

Note: bks all lower and upright stems with a double line of dark brown.

FLOWER BASKET ▼	DMC	ANCHOR	MADEIRA
◁ Yellow	741	304	0114
◆ Orange	721	324	0308
⊡ Ginger	781	365	2213
I Pale pink	761	49	0502
✱ Pink	3733	76	0505
• Pale magenta	603	62	0701
△ Warm pink	351	10	0214
↓ Blue	341	117	0901
S Pale green	3348	254	1409
O Green	3364	266	1513
↑ Light stone	3047	886	2205
◣ Stone	372	854	2110

Note: bks the right side of the basket with ginger, around the bow with pink, the stems with green, and around the base, left side and edge of the basket with stone.

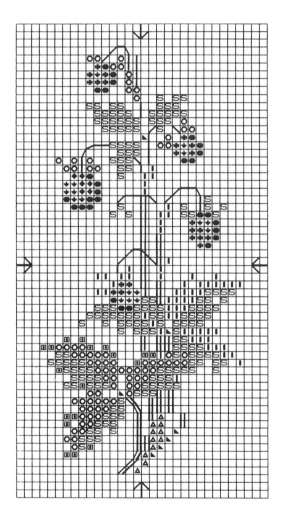

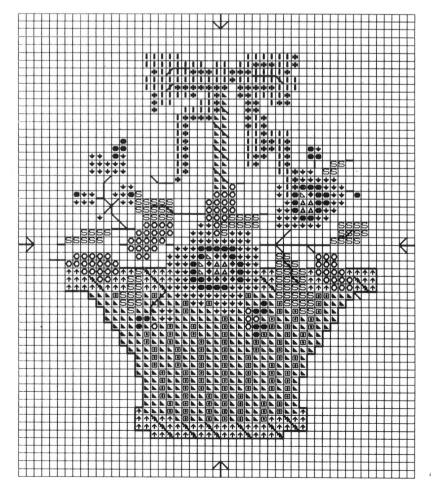

Wedding-Day Treasures

This exquisite ringbearer's cushion, embroidered with doves, flowers, hearts and the bride's and groom's initials, and surrounded with delicate floral borders and lace trim, is teamed with two charming well-wisher's confetti/rice bags. Edged and tied with ribbon bows, these little bags would make pretty purses after the wedding — looped on a sash in pocket-purse style — and all three pieces would become treasured mementoes of the day.

WEDDING-DAY TREASURES

YOU WILL NEED

For a Ringbearer's cushion measuring 25cm (10in) square (including lace trim):

*Two 20cm (8in) squares of white evenweave,
26-count linen or Davosa
Stranded embroidery cotton in the colours
given in the appropriate panel
76cm (30in) of white pre-gathered lace trim,
4cm (1½in) wide
20cm (8in) square cushion pad
Two 46cm (18in) lengths of parcel ribbon, one in
blue and one in pale pink
No26 tapestry needle
Matching sewing threads*

For the Well-wisher's confetti/rice bags,
each measuring approximately 13cm × 10cm
(5in × 4in):

*Two 33cm × 12cm (13in × 4½in) pieces of white,
26-count evenweave linen or Davosa
Stranded embroidery cotton in the colours
given in the appropriate panels
Two 90cm (1yd) lengths of satin ribbon, 12mm
(½in) wide, one in pale blue and one in pale pink
No26 tapestry needle
Matching sewing thread
Tracing paper*

●

THE RING-BEARER'S CUSHION

With the prepared fabric stretched in a hoop, see page 8, begin the embroidery, using two strands of thread in the needle and working one cross stitch over two threads of ground fabric throughout. Following the chart and colour key, begin with the inner border and finish with the outer border. Using 955, make an eye with a french knot, two stitches back from the beak, on each bird. Complete the embroidery and remove it from the hoop. Take out the basting stitches and steam press on the wrong side, if needed.

MAKING UP THE CUSHION

Using a tiny french seam, join the raw short edges of the lace trim together. Lay the lace on the embroidery, facing inward and with right sides together, and baste the edge of the lace to the outer edge of the fabric, just inside the 12mm (½in) seam allowance. Ease the gathers around the edges, allowing a little extra fullness at the corners. Machine stitch in place.

With right sides together, place the backing fabric on top. Baste and machine stitch around, leaving a 13cm (5in) opening in the middle of one side. Trim across the corners and turn the cover through to the right side.

Fold the lengths of parcel ribbon in half and stitch the folds to the centre of the cushion, in readiness for tying on the wedding rings.

Insert the cushion pad, turn in the edges of the opening and slipstitch to close.

THE HEART-SHAPED CONFETTI BAG

Fold the prepared fabric widthways in half and cut along the fold. Set one section (the back) aside, and on the other mark the centre both ways with basting stitches. Stretch the fabric in a hoop and, referring to the chart, complete the embroidery, using two strands of thread in the needle and working one cross stitch over two threads throughout. Steam press the finished embroidery on the wrong side.

MAKING UP THE BAG

Using a soft pencil, trace the outline of the heart and mark the centre lines, as on the chart. Lay the embroidery face down. Turn over the tracing and place it on the embroidery, with basting and pencil lines matching, then go over the outline to transfer it to the fabric. Working freehand, draw a second line 12mm (½in) outside, for the seam allowance, and cut out the fabric. Using this as a template, cut out the backing fabric.

Cut a 25cm (10in) length of ribbon for the handle, and put this to one side. Join the raw ends of the remaining ribbon together, using a tiny french seam. Pleat the ribbon and pin it to the right side of the embroidery, in the same way as the lace trim for the Ring-bearer's cushion. With the embroidery and backing fabric right sides together, machine stitch around the edge, leaving the opening, as marked on the chart.

Turn and hem a 6mm (¼in) double turning on the top edge of the backing.

For the handle, fold the remaining ribbon and attach the two ends inside the top front edge with a few back stitches, taken through the seam allowance. Make a buttonhole loop inside the hem opposite. Fill the bag with confetti, then thread the handle through the loop.

THE STRAIGHT-SIDED CONFETTI BAG

Following the diagram on page 51, fold the fabric widthways in half and mark the foldline with basting stitches. In the top section only, baste the vertical centre to give the positioning lines for the embroidery. Referring to the chart, complete the embroidery as for the heart-shaped bag.

MAKING UP THE BAG

With right sides together, fold the fabric widthways in half and baste the two sides. Machine stitch, using matching sewing thread. Trim the seams to 6mm (¼in) and press open. Make a 12mm (½in) double turning on the top edge; pin; baste, and hem to secure.

For the handle, cut 40cm (16in) of pink ribbon and tuck the ends inside the bag, catchstitching them to the centre front and back, about 3cm (1¼in) in from the edge (where the stitches will be hidden under the tied bow). Fold the remaining ribbon in half and attach it to the side of the bag, about 3cm (1¼in) down from the top edge. Fill the bag with confetti or rice and tie the ribbon in a bow to finish.

BLUE CONFETTI BAG ▼	DMC	ANCHOR	MADEIRA
○ Pale gold	677	886	2207
⊡ Yellow	744	301	0112
✦ Pale blue	3747	129	0901
● Blue	794	120	0907
△ Green	772	264	1604
✱ Grey green	504	213	1701

Leave open

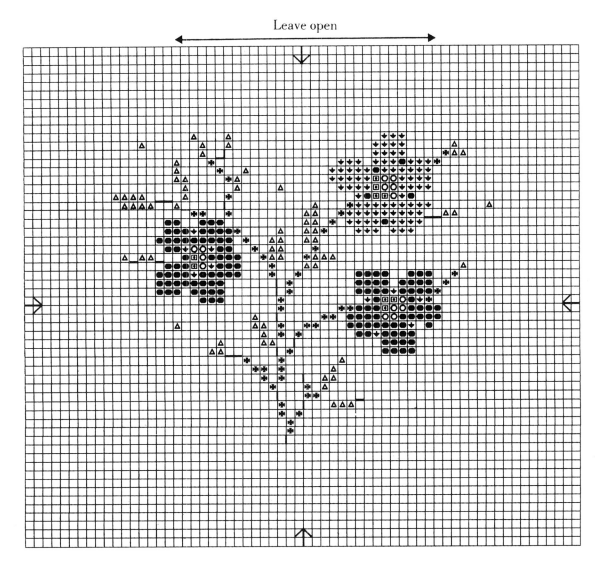

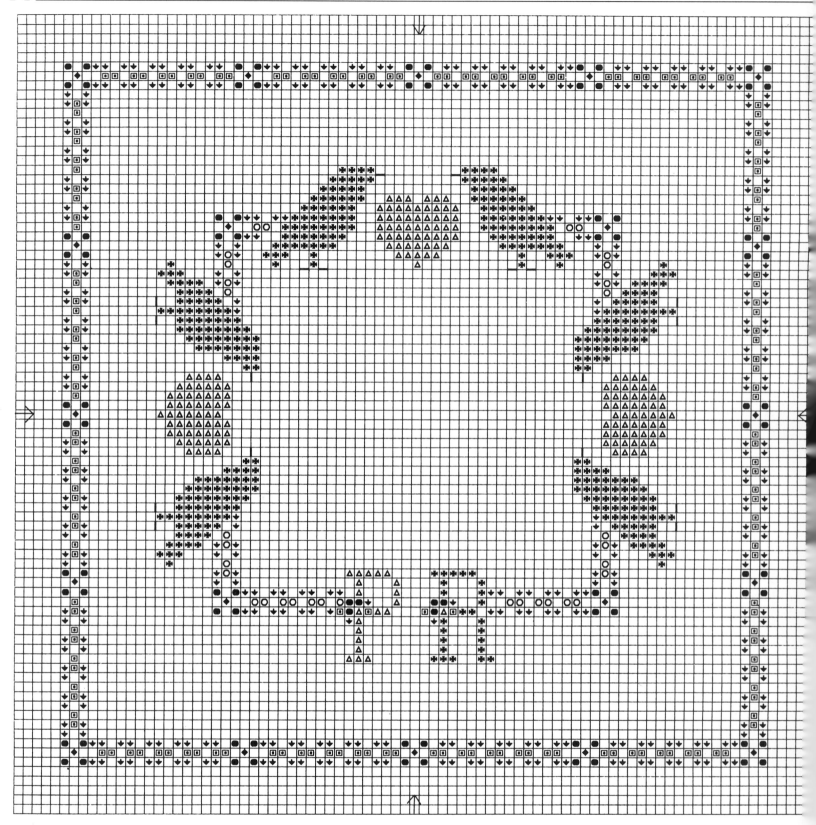

WEDDING RING PILLOW ▲

		DMC	ANCHOR	MADEIRA
◆	Yellow	677	886	2207
△	Pink	605	50	0613
●	Deep pink	963	271	0502
✹	Blue	3747	129	0901
⊡	Mint green	955	203	1210
↓	Yellow green	722	323	0307
○	Grey green	504	213	1701

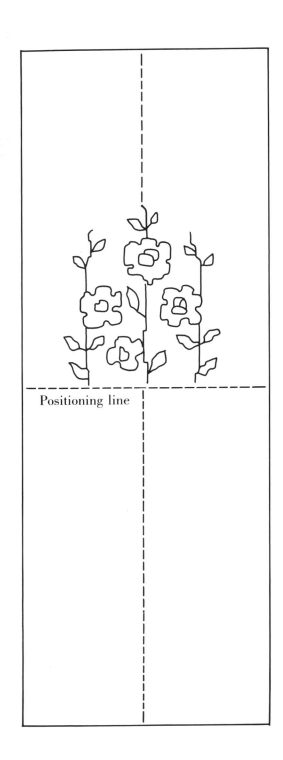

Positioning line

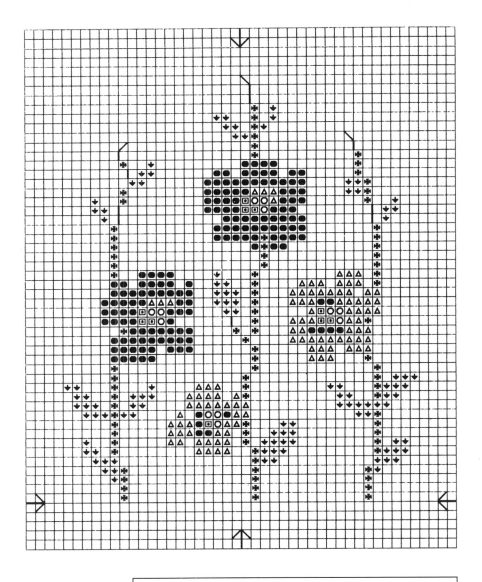

PINK CONFETTI			
BAG ▲	DMC	ANCHOR	MADEIRA
○ Pale gold	677	886	2207
⊡ Yellow	744	301	0112
△ Pale pink	605	50	0613
● Pink	962	52	0609
↓ Green	722	323	0307
✳ Grey green	504	213	1701

SAMPLERS AND PICTURES

Samplers have been part of our way of life for hundreds of years, but became popular as decorative pieces of work in the 19th century, when they were used in this way by the Victorians.

The selection shown here contains some in the traditional vein together with others that are more modern in feel.

If you prefer to embroider a picture, there is a wide selection from which to choose, including a panel of wild flower portraits, a bouquet of roses, and a charming study of poppies.

Rose Sampler

A midsummer day's dream is captured in this elegant rose sampler. 'How fair is the rose' showers praise, as rose garlands twine around the sampler. The romanticism of the rose is emphasized by the soft pink, mauve and blue shades of the basket of roses, which creates a charming focal point. Coolness and viridescence wait in the shadows of the olive, sage and lime green shades of the leaves.

ROSE SAMPLER

YOU WILL NEED

For the sampler, with a design area measuring
26.5cm × 31cm (10½in × 12¼in), or 154
stitches by 175 stitches, here in a frame
measuring 42.5cm × 46cm (17in × 18½in):

*36.5cm × 41cm (14½in × 16½in) of white,
14-count Aida fabric
Stranded embroidery cotton in the colours given
in the panel
No24 tapestry needle
Strong thread, for lacing across the back
Cardboard, for mounting, sufficient to fit in to the
frame recess
Frame of your choice*

●

THE EMBROIDERY

Prepare the fabric and stretch it in a frame as
explained on page 9. Following the chart, start the
embroidery at the centre of the design, using two
strands of embroidery cotton in the needle. Work
each stitch over one block of fabric in each
direction. Make sure that all the top crosses run in
the same direction and each row is worked into the
same holes as the top or bottom of the row before,
so that you do not leave a space between the rows.

To give the basket more definition, work the
outline in backstitch, with one strand of darkest
brown cotton in the needle.

The shades chosen would fit very well in a bedroom colour scheme, but the sampler would look
equally attractive if the colours were changed for
stronger shades of green for the leaves and perhaps
red and dark magenta for the roses.

MAKING UP

Gently steam press the work on the wrong side and
mount it as explained on page 10. When framing
the picture, consider using a double mount with the
darker of the shades on the inside, to give your
sampler extra depth. Do not prepare your embroidery by lacing it over the mounting cardboard until
you have chosen your frame and decided whether
you will also require a mount (double or single).
These decisions will all affect the amount of fabric
that you will wish to leave around the edges of the
embroidered area.

ROSE SAMPLER ◀	DMC	ANCHOR	MADEIRA
∕ Light pink	3689	66	0606
: Medium pink	3688	68	0605
⟨ Dark pink	3685	70	0514
⟩ Light mauve	211	342	0801
⟍ Medium mauve	210	109	0803
c̄ Dark mauve	208	111	0804
v Yellow	3078	292	0102
‡ Light blue	932	920	0907
+ Dark blue	311	148	1007
o Light green	369	213	1309
r Medium green	320	215	1311
s Dark green	319	217	1313
w Light brown	842	376	1910
x Medium brown	841	378	1911
z Dark brown	840	379	1912
Darkest brown*	938	381	2005

Darkest brown used for bks outline of basket only.

Poppy Picture and Frame

The bright red of fragile poppies growing among stems of bearded barley is used here to create a striking picture. To complete the effect, the same design has been used for an eye-catching surround for a favourite photograph.

POPPY PICTURE
AND FRAME

YOU WILL NEED

For the Poppy picture, measuring 27cm × 22cm
(10¾in × 8¾in) when framed:

*33cm × 27.5cm (13in × 11in) of cream,
18-count Aida
Stranded embroidery cotton in the colours given
in the panel
No26 tapestry needle
Strong thread, for lacing across the back when
mounting
Cardboard for mounting
Frame of your choice*

For the photograph frame, measuring
27cm × 22cm (10¾in × 8¾in), with an aperture
measuring 14cm × 9cm (5½in × 3½in):

*25.5cm × 20.5cm (10¼in × 8¼in) of white,
14-count perforated paper
Stranded embroidery cotton in the colours given
in the panel
No24 tapestry needle
25.5cm × 20.5cm (10¼in × 8¼in) of iron-on
interfacing
Frame of your choice*

●

THE EMBROIDERY

For the picture, prepare the fabric and mark the
horizontal and vertical centre lines with basting
stitches in a light-coloured thread. Stretch the
fabric in an embroidery frame, following the
instructions on page 9. Begin at the centre and
work out, using two strands of embroidery cotton in
the needle for both cross stitch and backstitching.
Gently steam press the finished embroidery.

For the frame, find the centre of the perforated
paper by counting the spaces between holes. Mark
this point with a soft pencil, and then count out to
a convenient starting point on the border. Use three
strands of embroidery cotton in the needle for both
cross stitch and backstitching. When you have
completed your design, cut out the central aperture. Mark the line first with a soft pencil and cut
with a sharp craft knife.

MOUNTING AND FRAMING

For the picture, mark the central horizontal and
vertical lines on the cardboard to be used for mounting and align these with the lines of basting stitches.
Lace the embroidery over the mount, following
the instructions on page 10, and remove basting
stitches. Set the mount in a frame of your choice.

For the frame, iron the interfacing to the back of
the embroidered perforated paper and then use a
craft knife to trim the interfacing to the same size,
including the aperture. Insert the embroidered
paper into the frame of your choice.

POPPY PICTURE

POPPY FRAME

Note: one skein of each colour will complete both designs, but if you are only making the frame you will not require the dark brown; poppy picture bks the stamens of the seed heads in black, barley whiskers and soil in fawn, highlights on the seed pod in yellowish green, lines separating the barley grains in cream, soil in dark brown, and poppy bud stems in green; for the frame bks barley whiskers in fawn, lines separating barley grains in cream, tip of barley leaf in pale green, and poppy bud stems in green.

POPPIES		DMC	ANCHOR	MADEIRA
	Cream*	746	275	0101
↑	Red	349	13	0212
⊠	Deep red	498	19	0511
◣	Maroon	902	897	0601
Ƴ	Light orange	608	330	0206
☐	Orange red	606	335	0209
■	Deep orange	900	333	0208
／	Deep salmon	3340	329	0301
⊠	Pale green	3053	859	1510
⊪	Green	3347	266	1408
◥	Medium green	3346	817	1407
▼	Dark green	3345	268	1406
⊟	Yellowish green	472	264	1414
◻	Fawn	372	887	2110
⊞	Dark brown	3031	905	2003
■	Black	310	403	Black

Botanical Sampler

Look through a text book on roses and, alongside the more familiar names of your favourite species, you will find their scientific names. In this design, the Latin names have been used as a frame for the beautiful blooms of a selection of our more traditional roses.
Set in a frame with an appropriate period air, this beautiful sampler will make an attractive focal point in any room.

Rosa xanthina

Rosa farren persetosa

Rosa spinosissima

Rosa rugosa

BOTANICAL SAMPLER

YOU WILL NEED

For the sampler, with a design area measuring 17cm × 23.5cm (6¾in × 9½in), or 103 stitches by 133 stitches, here in a frame measuring 27.5cm × 33cm (11in × 13in):

*27cm × 33.5cm (10¾in × 13¼in) of cream,
14-count Aida fabric
Stranded embroidery cotton in the colours given
in the panel
No24 tapestry needle
Strong thread, for lacing across the back
Cardboard, for mounting, sufficient to fit into the
frame recess
Frame of your choice*

•

THE EMBROIDERY

Prepare the fabric and stretch it in a frame as explained on page 9. Following the chart, start the embroidery at the centre of the design, using two strands of embroidery cotton in the needle. Work each stitch over one block of fabric in each direction. Make sure that all the top crosses run in the same direction and that each row is worked into the same holes as the top or bottom of the row before, leaving no spaces between the rows.

Make french knots for seeds in the bottom left-hand corner with six and three strands of light and medium green stranded cotton respectively, winding the cotton once around the needle and using the picture as a guide. Make the straight lines in backstitch with three strands of light green cotton.

Work the names around the outside in backstitch using two strands of dark brown cotton, and the branches with two strands of medium brown cotton.

MAKING UP

Gently steam press the work on the wrong side and mount as explained on page 10. Set your finished sampler in a traditional frame.

BOTANICAL SAMPLER ▶	DMC	ANCHOR	MADEIRA
≉ Light pink	605	50	0613
╱ Medium pink	604	60	0614
r Dark pink	603	62	0701
e Darkest pink	602	63	0702
− Light mauve	210	108	0803
⟩ Medium mauve	208	111	0804
$ Dark mauve	550	101	0714
% Light yellow	3078	292	0102
a Medium yellow	743	301	0113
o Dark yellow	742	302	0107
c Light green	3348	264	1409
x Medium green	3347	266	1408
= Dark green	937	268	1504
s Light brown	640	393	1905
\ Medium brown	841	378	1911
Dark brown*	938	381	2005

* Used for bks writing.

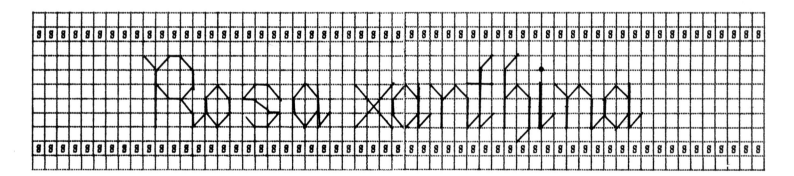

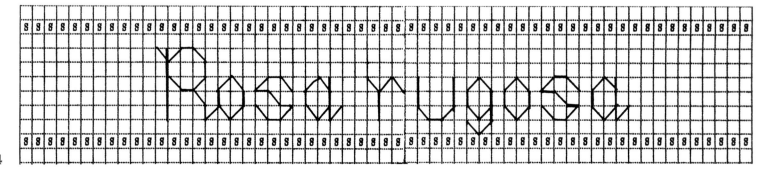

Rosa xanthina

Rosa rugosa

Traditional Sampler

This sampler would have looked perfectly at home hanging in a Victorian parlour around the turn of the century. A selection of traditional motifs of flowers and birds have been arranged to make this attractive design. Three of the motifs have been embroidered separately to make a delightful trio of pictures, or perhaps you would like to create a bell pull from the motifs, giving a truly Victorian flavour to your decor.

TRADITIONAL SAMPLER

YOU WILL NEED

For the sampler and each of the small pictures derived from it, you will need the following, plus the individual requirements specified below:

Stranded embroidery cotton in the colours given in the appropriate panel
No24 tapestry needle
Strong thread, for lacing across the back
Cardboard, for mounting, sufficient to fit into the frame recess
Frame of your choice

For the sampler, with a design area measuring 34cm × 25.5cm (13½in × 10¼in), or 183 stitches by 138 stitches, here in a frame measuring 40cm × 32.5cm (16in × 13in):

44cm × 35cm (17½in × 14in) of cream, 27-count Linda fabric

For the Rose picture, with a design area measuring 12cm × 13cm (4½in × 5in), or 64 stitches by 70 stitches, here in a frame measuring 18.5cm (7½in) square:

22cm × 23cm (8½in × 9in) of cream, 27-count Linda fabric

For the Cornflower picture, with a design area measuring 15cm × 11cm (6in × 4¼in), or 83 stitches by 59 stitches, here in a frame measuring 21cm × 16.5cm (8¼in × 6½in):

25cm × 21cm (10in × 8¼in) of cream, 27-count Linda fabric

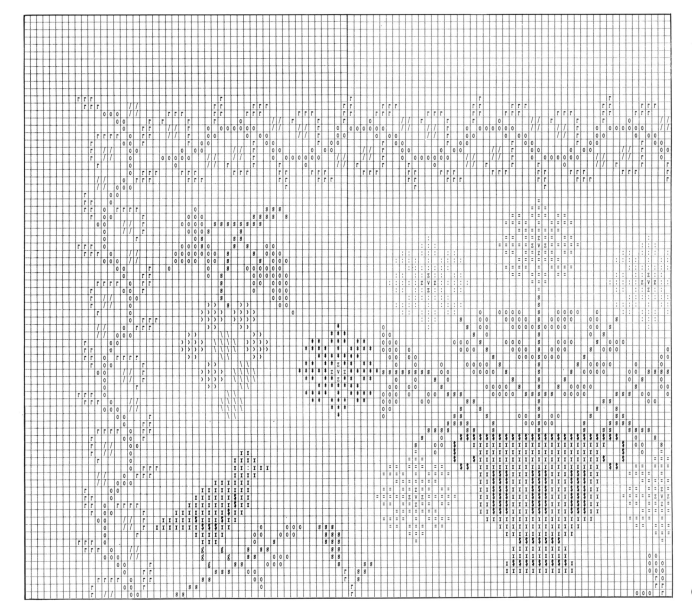

CHART 1

For the Bird picture, with a design area measuring 11cm × 8cm (4¼n × 3in), or 59 stitches by 44 stitches, here in a frame measuring 16.5cm × 13.5cm (6½in × 5¼in):

21cm × 18cm (8¼in × 7¼in) of cream, 27-count Linda fabric

•

THE EMBROIDERY

For each design, prepare the linen and stretch in a frame as explained on page 9. Following the chart, start the embroidery at the centre of the design, using two strands of embroidery cotton in the needle. Embroider each stitch over two threads of fabric in each direction. Make sure that all the top crosses run in the same direction and each row is worked into the same holes as the row before so that you do not leave a space between the rows. Work the butterfly feelers with two strands of dark brown cotton in backstitch.

MAKING UP

Gently steam press the work on the wrong side and mount it as explained on page 10. To retain the traditional feel of the sampler, choose a simple wooden frame without a cardboard mount.

NOTE

The sampler has been divided into four charts, each showing a quarter. The key and Charts 3 and 4 are on pages 72-3.

CHART 2

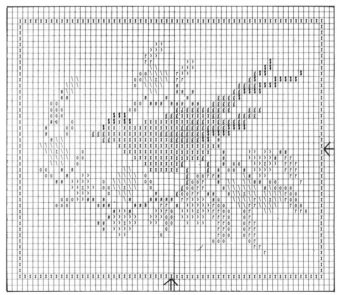

BIRD ▲		DMC	ANCHOR	MADEIRA
＼	Light mauve	341	117	0901
＜	Dark mauve	340	118	0902
g	Gold	834	874	2204
z	Dark yellow	725	298	0113
‡	Light blue	3325	976	1002
o	Light green	471	265	1502
r	Medium green	988	244	1402
s	Dark green	986	246	1404
x	Light brown	612	832	2002
$	Dark brown	370	856	2201

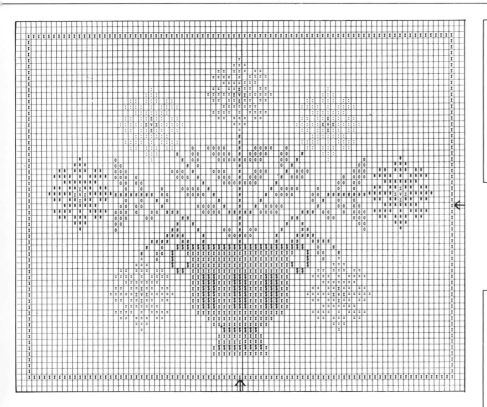

CORNFLOWER ◄		DMC	ANCHOR	MADEIRA
v	Light yellow	727	293	0110
z	Dark yellow	725	306	0108
‡	Light blue	3325	976	1002
:	Medium blue	334	977	1003
=	Dark blue	312	979	1005
o	Light green	471	265	1502
s	Dark green	986	246	1404
x	Light brown	612	832	2002
$	Dark brown	370	856	2201

ROSE ▼		DMC	ANCHOR	MADEIRA
%	Pale magenta	3609	85	0710
v	Light yellow	727	295	0111
z	Dark yellow	725	298	0113
o	Light green	471	265	1502
r	Medium green	988	244	1402
s	Dark green	986	246	1404
x	Light brown	612	832	2002
$	Dark brown	370	856	2201

TRADITIONAL SAMPLER		DMC	ANCHOR	MADEIRA
∕	Light pink	224	894	0813
〈	Dark pink	3721	896	0811
＼	Light mauve	341	117	0901
〉	Dark mauve	340	118	0902
%	Pale magenta	3609	85	0710
v	Light yellow	727	295	0111
z	Dark yellow	725	298	0113
g	Gold	834	874	2204
‡	Light blue	3325	379	1912
:	Medium blue	334	977	1003
=	Dark blue	312	979	1005
o	Light green	471	265	1502
r	Medium green	988	244	1402
s	Dark green	986	246	1404
x	Light brown	612	832	2002
$	Dark brown	370	856	2201

CHART 3

CHART 1 | CHART 2
CHART 3 | CHART 4

CHART 4

Summer Picture

This bouquet of peach and pink roses
is just as fresh as the moment it was
picked on a balmy summer's day.
The subtle shades of the roses make
this picture an ideal focal point for
anyone fond of pastel shades.
Alternatively, you might choose to
embroider the roses in shades of dark
pink and red to give warmth and
vibrance to the design.
The design has been shown here
as a picture, but you could, of
course, make it into a cushion cover,
if you prefer.

SUMMER PICTURE

YOU WILL NEED

For the Summer picture, with a design area measuring 19cm (7½in) square, or 110 stitches by 108 stitches, here in a frame measuring 36cm (14½in) square:

29cm (11½in) of white, 14-count Aida fabric
Stranded embroidery cotton in the colours given in the panel
No24 tapestry needle
Strong thread, for lacing across the back
Cardboard, for mounting, sufficient to fit into the frame recess
Frame and mount of your choice

•

THE EMBROIDERY

Prepare the fabric and stretch it in a frame as explained on page 9. Following the chart, start the embroidery at the centre of the design, using two strands of embroidery cotton in the needle. Work each stitch over one block of fabric in each direction. Make sure that all the top crosses run in the same direction and each row is worked into the same holes as the top or bottom of the row before, so that you do not leave a space between the rows.

MAKING UP

Gently steam press the work on the wrong side and mount it as explained on page 10. Choose a mount and frame to match your colour scheme.

SUMMER PICTURE ▶		DMC	ANCHOR	MADEIRA
‡	Light pink	3689	66	0606
/	Medium pink	3688	68	0605
r	Dark pink	3687	69	0604
e	Darkest pink	3685	70	0514
%	Light peach	948	778	0306
a	Medium peach	754	868	0305
o	Dark peach	353	6	0304
n	Darkest peach	352	9	0303
c	Light green	3348	264	1409
x	Medium green	3347	266	1408
=	Dark green	937	268	1504
s	Light brown	950	882	2309
@	Dark brown	407	914	2312

Flowery Alphabet Sampler

The treatment of traditional motifs and an alphabet in pastel colours bring this sampler up to date. The border of carnations can easily be extended to make space for your own words underneath the alphabet, or perhaps you could use the space filled here by the letters of the alphabet to write your own message.

This sampler can easily be adapted by using alternative shades of cotton.

FLOWERY ALPHABET SAMPLER

YOU WILL NEED

For the Bordered Alphabet sampler, with a design area measuring 26cm × 15cm (10¼in × 6in), or 144 stitches by 85 stitches, here in a frame measuring 36cm × 25cm (14½in × 10in):

36cm × 25cm (14in × 10in) of cream, 14-count Aida fabric
Stranded embroidery cotton in the colours given in the panel
No24 tapestry needle
Strong thread, for lacing across the back
Cardboard, for mounting, sufficient to fit into the frame recess
Frame of your choice

●

THE EMBROIDERY

Prepare the fabric and stretch it in a frame as explained on page 9. Following the chart, start the embroidery at the centre of the design, using two strands of embroidery cotton in the needle. Work each stitch over one block of fabric in each direction. Make sure that all the top crosses run in the same direction and that each row is worked into the same holes as the top or bottom of the row before so that you do not leave a space between the rows.

MAKING UP

Gently steam press the work on the wrong side and mount it as explained on page 10. Choose a mount and frame to complement your embroidery colours.

FLOWERY ALPHABET ▶		DMC	ANCHOR	MADEIRA
‡	Light pink	3689	66	0606
–	Dark pink	3688	68	0605
o	Pale magenta	3609	85	0710
s	Light mauve	211	108	0801
x	Dark mauve	210	109	0803
‹	Light green	369	213	1309
=	Dark green	368	214	1310
%	Brown	841	378	1911

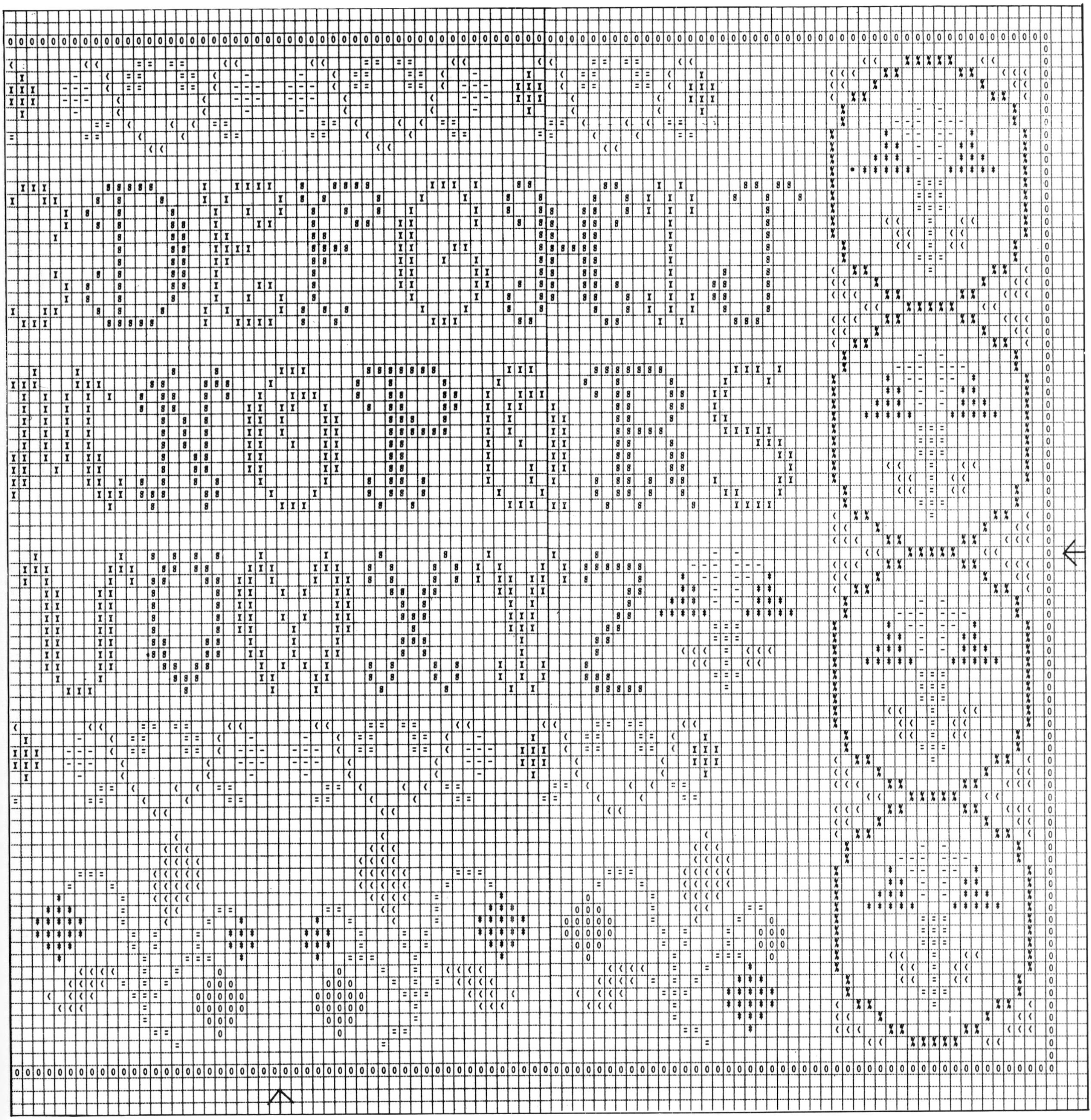

Cottage Garden

Walk down the pathway of this English cottage garden and take a step back in time. In your imagination, smell the sweet scent of lavender and absorb the colours and peacefulness of a bygone era. The rambling roses around the cottage door are embroidered with clusters of french knots to give extra depth and texture to this nostalgic design. It has been set in a deep frame, but an alternative idea would be to surround it with a double mount, to add to the sense of perspective.

COTTAGE GARDEN

YOU WILL NEED

For the Cottage Garden, with a design area measuring 19.5cm × 15cm (7¾in × 6in), or 119 stitches by 85 stitches, here in a frame measuring 23cm × 18.5cm (9in × 7½in):

30cm × 25cm (12in × 10in) of white, 14-count Aida fabric
Stranded embroidery cotton in the colours given in the panel
No24 tapestry needle
Strong thread, for lacing across the back
Cardboard for mounting, sufficient to fit in the frame recess
Frame and mount of your choice

●

THE EMBROIDERY

Prepare the piece of fabric and stretch it in a frame as explained on page 9. Following the chart, start the embroidery at the centre of the design, using two strands of embroidery cotton in the needle. Work each stitch over a block of fabric in each direction. Make sure that all the top crosses run in the same direction and each row is worked into the same holes as the top or bottom of the row before, so that you do not leave a space between the rows.

Using backstitch, work all the outlines and markings with one strand of dark green cotton. Work the roses in clusters of medium and dark coloured pink french knots, using six strands of cotton in the needle and winding the cotton around the needle either once or twice, varying this so that some clusters of roses stand out more than others, to create a three-dimensional effect.

MAKING UP

Steam press the work on the wrong side and mount it as explained on page 10. Choose a mount and frame that are in keeping with the 'Olde Worlde' charm of the picture.

COTTAGE GARDEN		DMC	ANCHOR	MADEIRA			DMC	ANCHOR	MADEIRA
╱	Light pink	776	73	0606	c	Cream	746	275	0101
:	Medium pink	894	26	0408	+	Light gold	676	887	2208
<	Dark pink	891	29	0412	n	Medium gold	729	890	2209
╲	Light mauve	210	108	0803	g	Dark gold	680	901	2210
>	Medium mauve	208	111	0804	v	Yellow	743	301	0113
%	Dark mauve	550	101	0714	‡	Light blue	799	130	0910

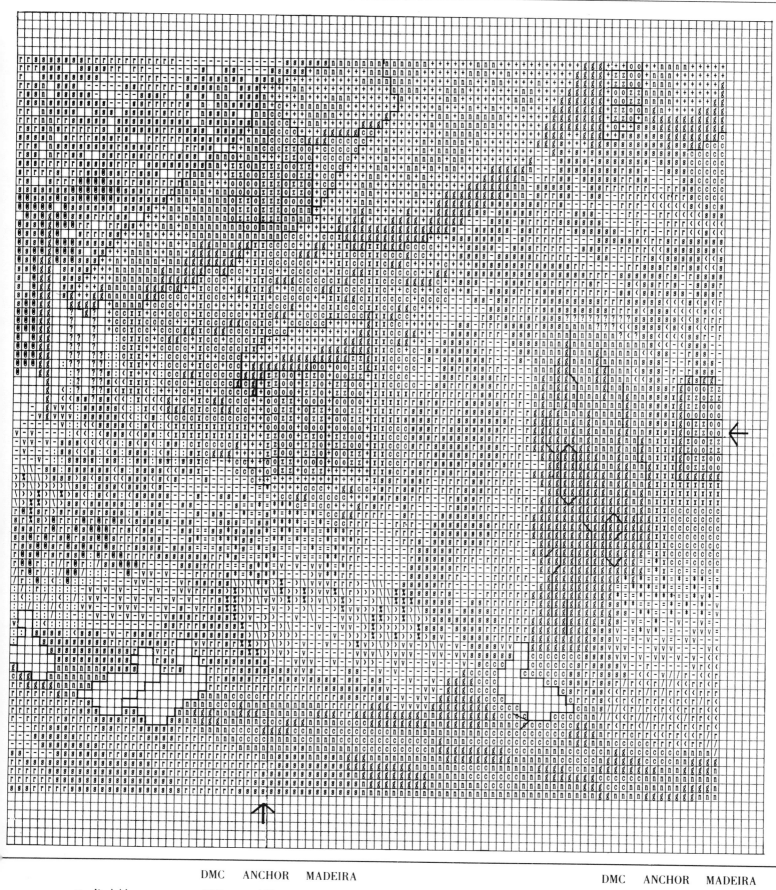

		DMC	ANCHOR	MADEIRA			DMC	ANCHOR	MADEIRA
=	Dark blue	798	131	0911	?	Dark brown	829	906	2106
−	Light green	3348	264	1409	o	Light grey	762	234	1804
r	Medium green	3347	266	1408	z	Dark grey	414	399	1801
s	Dark green	3345	268	1406					
@	Darkest green	936	263	1507					
x	Light brown	434	365	2009					

A Panel of Flowers

This panel of wayside flowers, with their delicate hues, will bring a touch of the countryside to your home. You might choose to mount it in a frame, as shown, but the design is so adaptable that you could take any section and turn it into a smaller picture, or indeed make a set of flower portraits, in matching frames, to decorate a guest bedroom, or perhaps a staircase.

A PANEL OF FLOWERS

YOU WILL NEED

For this panel, here with a frame measurement of
39.5cm × 37cm (15¾in × 14½in):

*47cm × 43.5cm (19in × 17½in) of cream,
18-count Aida
Stranded embroidery cotton in the colours given
in the panel
No26 tapestry needle*

*Strong cardboard, for the mount, sufficient to fit
into the frame recess
Strong thread, for lacing across the back when
mounting
Picture frame of your choice*

*NOTE To complete the sampler, you will only
need one skein each of every colour listed in the
combined six charts, with the exception of green
(3346/817/1407), for which you will
require two skeins.*

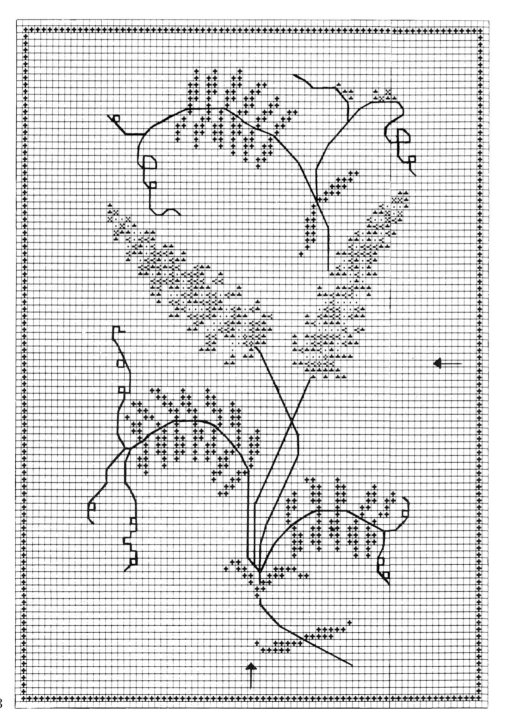

Chart 1 Tufted Vetch

TUFTED VETCH ◀		DMC	ANCHOR	MADEIRA
x	Pink	3608	86	0709
·	Pale mauve	211	342	0801
-:	Medium mauve	554	97	0711
⊥	Deep mauve	553	98	0712
∴	Light green	3347	266	1408
+	Green	3346	817	1407

Note: use light green for bks.

THE EMBROIDERY

Prepare the edges of the fabric in the usual way. The six panels of the design are shown on separate charts, so the centre lines of each must be marked. Start by marking the horizontal and vertical centre lines of the fabric with basting stitches. The border around each flower study measures 99 stitches (in total) down each side and 75 stitches (in total) along the top and bottom, and there are two threads between each border. You may find it easier to work out where to place the centre basting lines if you lightly mark the border outlines on the back of the fabric with a soft pencil.

With the fabric held in a frame (see page 9), work from the centre point of each chart to complete the panels one by one. Start with the two central panels, top and bottom, and check that you have the positioning correct before going on to complete the four corner panels. Use two strands of embroidery cotton in the needle for both the cross stitch and the backstitching, with the exceptions of fine details, such as stamens, which are stitched with one thread, as on the charts.

When you have completed the embroidery, gently steam press it on the wrong side. Leave the two central lines of basting stitches in place, but remove those at either side.

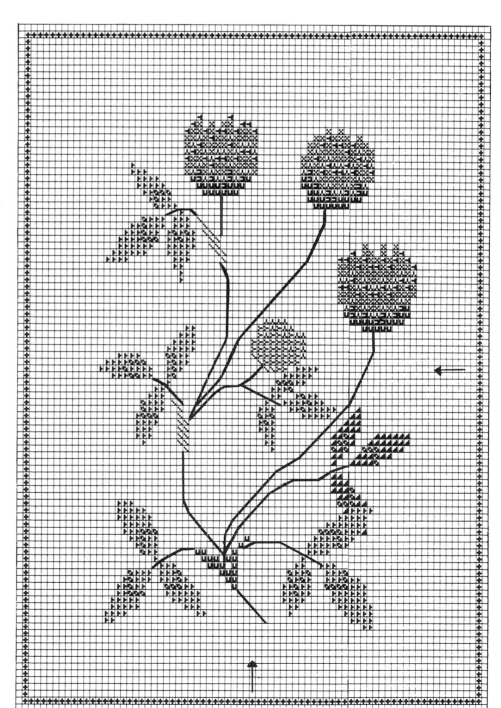

Chart 2 Red Clover

RED CLOVER ▶	DMC	ANCHOR	MADEIRA
⌁ Pale pink	3609	85	0710
✗ Pink	3608	86	0709
⊣ Deep pink	3607	87	0708
⊐ Purplish red	315	896	0810
⏚ Silver green	524	858	1511
∴ Yellowish green	472	264	1414
∵ Pale moss green	734	279	1610
⊔ Medium moss green	733	280	1611
⊢ Medium green	3363	262	1602
◢ Dark green	936	269	1507

Note: use medium green for bks.

MOUNTING THE PANEL

Mark the central horizontal and vertical lines on the cardboard and align these with the lines of basting stitches. Lace the embroidery over the mount, following the instructions on page 10, and remove basting stitches.

Set the mount in a frame of your choice. The one used here was intentionally selected for its unobtrusive simplicity, but a narrow silvered frame might be equally effective.

As an alternative idea, the flower portraits might be embroidered and framed individually to make a set of pictures or even scatter cushions.

The flowers chosen – tufted vetch (*Vicia cracca*), red clover (*Trifolium pratense*), chicory (*Cichorium intybus*), rosebay willowherb (*Epilobium angustifolium*), harebell (*Campanula rotundifolia*) and field scabious (*Knautia arvensis*) – are all ones that you might find by the wayside when walking on a summer's afternoon.

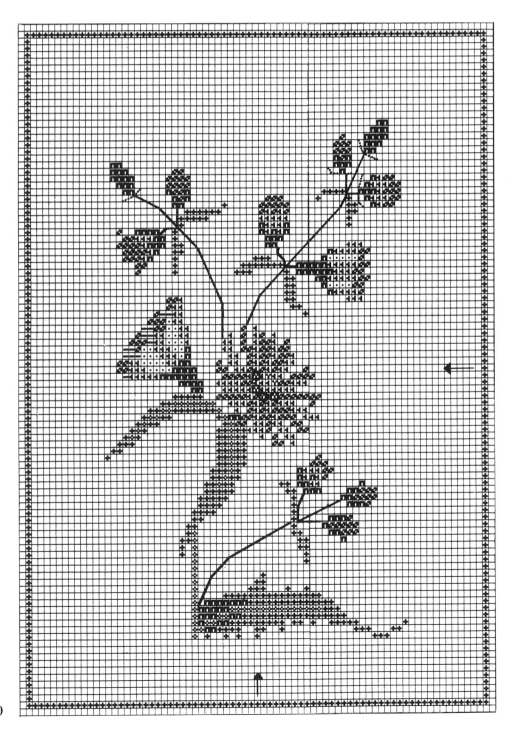

Chart 3 Chicory

CHICORY ◄	DMC	ANCHOR	MADEIRA
⊤ Cream	746	275	0101
· Pale mauve	211	342	0801
◢ Mauve	210	108	0802
Deep mauve*	553	98	0712
— Pale blue	341	117	0901
▪ Blue	340	118	0902
∴ Light green	3347	266	1408
+ Green	3346	817	1407
⊓ Dark green	520	862	1514

Note: bks bracts in dark green, flower centre in deep mauve*, and main stems in light green.

Chart 4 Rosebay Willowherb

ROSEBAY WILLOWHERB ▶	DMC	ANCHOR	MADEIRA
Cream*	746	275	0101
⌡ Pale pink	3609	85	0710
✗ Pink	3608	86	0709
⊣ Deep pink	3607	87	0708
⊐ Purplish red	315	896	0810
∴ Light green	3347	266	1408
┏ Moss green	522	859	1513
├ Medium green	3363	262	1602
⊓ Dark green	520	862	1514

Note: bks flower centres and stamens in cream, main stem and style in light green, top of seed pod and stalks in deep pink, and bud and flower stalks in pink.

HAREBELL ▼		DMC	ANCHOR	MADEIRA
I	Pale blue	794	120	0907
⊥	Medium blue	793	121	0906
╱	Dark blue	792	940	0905
∴	Light green	3347	266	1408
+	Green	3346	817	1407

Note: bks bracts in green and flower and leaf stems in light green.

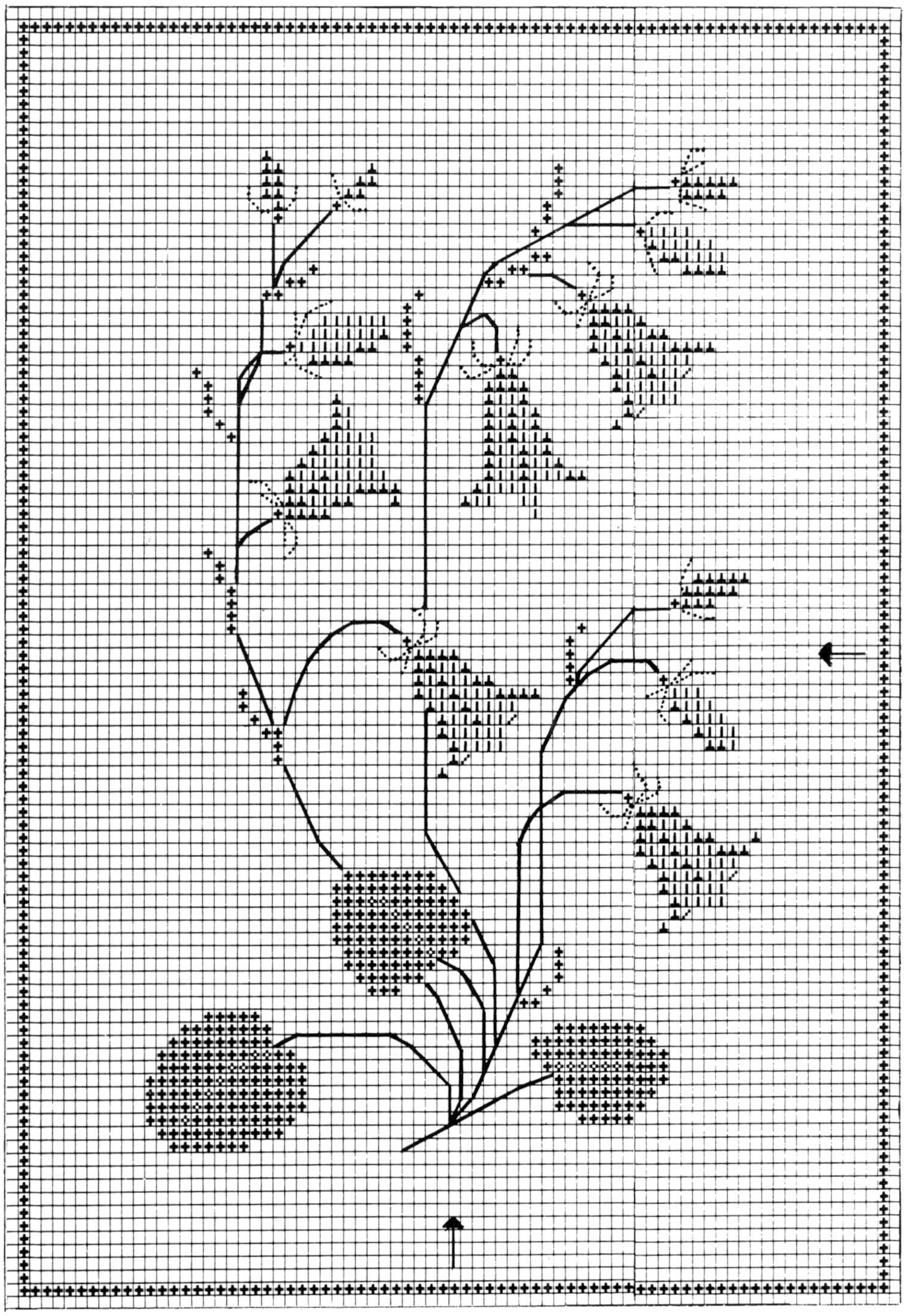

Chart 5 Harebell

1 Tufted Vetch	2 Red Clover	3 Chicory
4 Rosebay Willowherb	5 Harebell	6 Field Scabious

FIELD SCABIOUS ▼	DMC	ANCHOR	MADEIRA
.¦. Pale pink	3609	85	0710
· Pale mauve	211	342	0801
⊣ Mauve	210	108	0802
−: Medium mauve	554	97	0711
∟ Purplish red*	315	896	0810
⊏ Pale blue	828	158	1101
Blue*	340	118	0902
∴ Light green	3347	266	1408
+ Green	3346	817	1407
⊤ Dark green	3345	268	1406

Note: use purplish red* to separate petals and bks stamens, and blue* for bks outlining flower centre, separating it from the petals.

Chart 6 Field Scabious

QUICK AND EASY GIFTS

One of the delights of cross stitch is that it offers the opportunity to please friends and family with charming handmade gifts. A bookmark makes a thoughtful gift for a friend in hospital, floral guest towels are perfect presents, small gifts such as scented sachets or a pretty pincushion will be used and treasured for years. Even the eglantine and bramble pictures, although they are delicately and subtly shaded, are small in scale and therefore quick to embroider.

Gift Tags and Bookmark

These little hand-made tags will enhance any gift by adding that special personal touch. In this group of designs, the wild pansy and the red campion are accompanied by the meadow cranesbill, a member of the geranium family.

GIFT TAGS AND BOOKMARK

YOU WILL NEED

For the Meadow Cranesbill bookmark, measuring
20.5cm × 7cm (8in × 3in):

*25cm × 11.5cm (10in × 4½in) of white, 14-count
perforated paper
20.5cm × 7.5cm (8in × 3in) of iron-on
interfacing
50cm (20in) of lilac ribbon, 6mm (¼in) wide
Stranded embroidery cotton in the colours given
in the appropriate panel
No24 tapestry needle*

For the Red Campion gift tag, measuring
9.5cm × 5cm (3¾in × 2in):

*19cm × 5cm (7½in × 2in) of white, 14-count
perforated paper
19cm × 5cm (7½in × 2in) of parchment paper,
for the inside
Stranded embroidery cotton in the colours given
in the appropriate panel
No24 tapestry needle*

For either the Meadow Cranesbill or the Wild
Pansy gift tag, each measuring 5cm (2in):

*10cm (4in) of cream, 22-count Aida fabric
Stranded embroidery cotton in the colours given
in the appropriate panel
No26 tapestry needle
Gift tag (for suppliers, see page 160)*

THE EMBROIDERY

For the designs embroidered on perforated paper, use three strands of thread in the needle. Find the centre of the bookmark paper by counting the spaces between the holes. Fold the paper for the tag in half, and find the centre of the front half only. In either case, mark the centre with a soft pencil, which can be rubbed out later. Begin from the centre point of the pattern and work outward.

The design for the meadow cranesbill tag is simply the top flower from the bookmark design. For this and the wild pansy tag, use one strand of thread in the needle for both cross stitch and back-stitch, and embroider from the centre. Gently steam press the embroidery on the wrong side.

FINISHING THE BOOKMARK

Centre the interfacing on the wrong side of the book-mark, then iron it in place. Trim around the border of the design, leaving an edging of two perforations. You may find it easier to mark your cutting line with a soft pencil before you start.

Cut the ribbon in half. Gather along the edge of one piece and tighten it into a rosette. Fold the other length in half to make two streamers and stitch the fold to the lower edge of the bookmark. Glue or stitch the rosette in place over the streamers.

MAKING THE GIFT TAGS

For the red campion gift tags, use all-purpose adhesive to glue the parchment paper to the back of the embroidered paper. Fold the tag in half.

For the meadow cranesbill or wild pansy tag, trim around the design until the fabric measures 4.5cm (1¾in) square. Open the tag and centre the design in the aperture, then secure according to the manufac-turer's instructions.

RED CAMPION ◀		DMC	ANCHOR	MADEIRA
I	Pale pink	3609	85	0710
∴	Pink	3608	86	0709
T	Deep pink	3607	87	0708
Ц	Purplish red	315	896	0810
−	Pale green	3348	264	1409
Y	Green	3347	266	1408
+	Dark green	3346	817	1407

Note: bks stalks and flower centre in green.

MEADOW CRANESBILL ▶		DMC	ANCHOR	MADEIRA
·	Pale mauve	211	342	0801
⊥	Mauve	210	108	0802
I	Pale lavender blue	341	117	0901
x	Blue	340	118	0902
÷	Medium blue	794	120	0907
♫	Lime green	471	266	1501
⌐	Green	3363	262	1602
+	Dark green	501	878	1704
—	Fawn	613	831	2109
Υ	Greenish brown	611	898	2107
Ц	Dark brown	898	360	2006
■	Black	310	403	Black

Note: bks outline the centre of the upper flower in black, the petals of the lower flower in blue, seed pods in dark brown and stems and centre of upper flower in green; for the gift tag, buy only those colours indicated on the chart.

WILD PANSY ▼		DMC	ANCHOR	MADEIRA
☐	White*	White	2	White
—	Light mauve	554	97	0711
⌐	Medium mauve	552	101	0713
x	Dark mauve	550	102	0714
·	Yellow	726	295	0109
+	Dark green	3346	817	1407
■	Black	310	403	Black

Note: outline flower centres in white.*

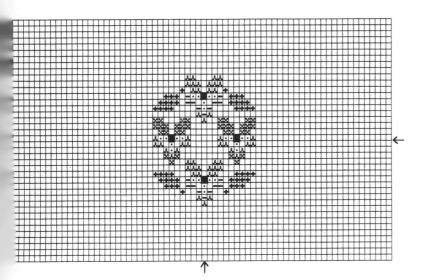

Small and Beautiful

These little samplers make an
excellent introduction to cross stitch.
The projects are small, and quick to
complete, but provide the stitcher
with an attractive first embroidery.

SMALL AND BEAUTIFUL

YOU WILL NEED

For Love is Kind, with a design area measuring 14.5cm × 17.5cm (5¾in × 7in), or 81 stitches by 97 stitches, here in a frame measuring 27cm × 30cm (10¾in × 12in):

24cm × 28cm (9½in × 11in) of cream, 14-count Aida fabric
Stranded embroidery cotton in the colours given in the appropriate panel
No24 tapestry needle
Strong thread, for lacing across the back
Cardboard, for mounting, sufficient to fit into the frame recess
Frame of your choice

For Home Sweet Home, with a design area measuring 17.5cm × 14cm (7in × 5½in), or 97 stitches by 77 stitches, here in a frame measuring 30.5cm × 26cm (12¼in × 10½in):

28cm × 24cm (11in × 9½in) of cream, 14-count Aida fabric
Stranded embroidery cotton in the colours given in the appropriate panel
No24 tapestry needle
Strong thread, for lacing across the back
Cardboard, for mounting, sufficient to fit into the frame recess
Frame of your choice

THE EMBROIDERY

Prepare the fabric and stretch it in a frame as explained on page 9. Following the appropriate chart, start the embroidery at the centre of the design, using two strands of embroidery cotton in the needle. Work each stitch over one block of fabric in each direction. Make sure that all the top crosses run in the same direction and that each row is worked into the same holes as the top or bottom of the row before so that you do not leave a space between the rows.

The bow and stalks on the *Love is Kind* sampler are worked in backstitch with two strands of green cotton, and the roses on the *Home Sweet Home* sampler are outlined with one strand of dark green cotton.

MAKING UP

Gently steam press the work on the wrong side and mount it as explained on page 10. The samplers could be framed as a matching pair or as two separate projects. The pine frames seen here complement the soft peach shades used for the embroideries, but these gentle shades could be exchanged for more vibrant colours to give a stronger feel to the designs.

Both samplers would look equally attractive stitched on an 11-count Aida fabric, which is particularly easy for a beginner to use. Remember that you may need extra stranded cotton for a design worked on an 11-count Aida because the stitches are bigger.

The *Love is Kind* sampler could be used as a small wedding sampler if the initials of the bride and groom were added, together with the date.

HOME SWEET HOME ◄		DMC	ANCHOR	MADEIRA
=	Pink	3688	68	0605
‹	Light peach	353	9	0304
+	Dark peach	352	10	0303
s	Light green	3052	844	1509
x	Dark green	319	218	1313
%	Brown	640	393	1905

LOVE IS KIND ►		DMC	ANCHOR	MADEIRA
c	Ecru	Ecru	926	Ecru
‹	Light peach	758	9575	0403
+	Dark peach	352	10	0303
x	Green	368	214	1310
%	Light brown	841	378	1911
=	Dark brown	829	906	2106

103

Pins and Needles

The vivid blue cornflower (*Centaurea cyanus*) provides a bold design for a pincushion. The diminutive and paler blue flowers of the forget-me-not (*Myosotis arvensis*) are used for the needlecase. These flowers have a yellow centre and are often a delicate pink in bud.

PINS AND NEEDLES

YOU WILL NEED

For the Forget-me-not needlecase, measuring
12.5cm × 11.5cm (5in × 4½in):

*33cm × 16.5cm (13in × 6½in) of cream,
18-count Aida fabric
27.5cm × 14cm (11in × 5½in) of satin lining fabric
25cm × 11.5cm (10in × 4½in) of heavyweight
iron-on interfacing
23cm × 9cm (9in × 3½in) of cream felt
45cm (18in) of matching ribbon, 6mm (¼in) wide
Stranded embroidery cotton in the colours given
in the appropriate panel
No26 tapestry needle*

For the Cornflower pincushion, measuring
10cm (4in) in diameter:

*23cm (9in) square of cream, 18 count Aida fabric
Stranded embroidery cotton in the colours given
in the appropriate panel
No26 tapestry needle
Pincushion base and pad (for suppliers, see
page 160)*

•

THE EMBROIDERY

For the needlecase, first fold the fabric in two, to
measure 16.5cm (6½) square. With the fold on the
left, measure in 2.5cm (1in) from each raw edge
and mark the upper surface of the fabric at the top,
bottom and right-hand side with basting stitches.
The centre of the area enclosed by the fold and
basting lines is the centre point of the design.

For each design, prepare the fabric and set it in a
hoop (see page 8). Embroider the design, using two
strands of thread in the needle for both the cross

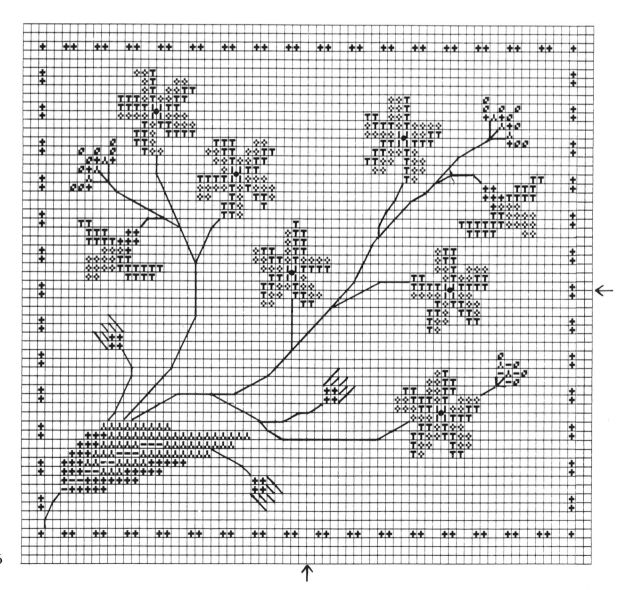

stitch and the backstitching. Gently press the finished embroidery on the wrong side.

FINISHING

For the needlecase, trim the fabric to measure
27.5cm × 14cm (11in × 5½in). Make and press
a 12mm (½in) turning on all sides, mitring the
corners. Slide the interfacing under the turnings and
iron it in place.

Turn under 12mm (½in) all around the lining
and hem it to cover the interfacing. Attach the felt to
the inside of the case by lightly stitching down the
centre. Tie the ribbon into a bow to trim the spine.

For the pincushion, use a plate or similar round
guide to trim the fabric to a 19cm (7½in) circle.
Stitching 12mm (½in) from the edge, run a line of
gathering stitches around the fabric. Place it over the
pincushion dome and tighten until it fits snugly.
Secure the thread firmly. Place the dome in the
wooden base and screw firmly into position.

FORGET-ME-NOT ◀		DMC	ANCHOR	MADEIRA
I	Yellow	307	289	0104
∴	Pale blue	794	120	0907
T	Blue	799	145	0910
↘	Purplish blue	340	118	0902
−	Pale green	3348	264	1409
↥	Green	3347	266	1408
+	Dark green	3346	817	1407
	Light brown*	680	901	2210

Note: bks flower centres in light brown, stems in dark green and
buds in purplish blue.*

CORNFLOWER ▼		DMC	ANCHOR	MADEIRA
·	Pale mauve	210	108	0802
⊔	Light navy	336	150	1007
I	Pale blue	341	117	0901
∴	Blue	340	118	0902
T	Dark blue	793	121	0906
↘	Green	3347	266	1408
+	Dark green	3345	268	1406

Bordered Guest Towels

Plain linen guest towels are decorated with simple floral motifs, repeated in sequence across one short edge only. Instead of embroidering across the full width, you may prefer to stitch a single motif in each corner of the towel.

To embroider other towelling, first cross stitch the design on a band of evenweave fabric and then hem it in place over the towelling pile.

BORDERED GUEST TOWELS

YOU WILL NEED

For two Guest towels, each measuring
62cm × 37cm (24½in × 14½in):

*Two prepared 26-count guest towels, which can be
purchased from specialist suppliers (see page 160);
alternatively, for applying a band to thick-pile
towelling, you will need 26-count evenweave
fabric, such as Linda, the width of the towel by
8cm (3in) deep, plus turnings on all sides
Stranded embroidery cotton in the colours
given in the panels
No26 tapestry needle
Matching sewing thread for applied band
Narrow lace edging (optional)*

•

THE EMBROIDERY

Embroidering a prepared guest towel is a relatively
easy operation, especially with these repeated
motifs – the most important consideration is to
make sure that you balance the repeats correctly,
starting from the centre.

At the end of the towel to be embroidered, begin
by basting the centre vertically (either count the
threads or measure precisely, and mark with a pin).
The line should ideally be about 15cm (6in) long.
Next, baste the base line across the towel, placing
this line 6cm (2½in) up from the hemstitching of
the fringed edge.

On both designs, work one cross stitch over two
threads of ground fabric. Following the chart and
using two strands of thread in the needle throughout, complete the first half of the border, beginning
in the marked centre. Complete the second half by
repeating the design, again stitching out from the
centre. If you work this way, the finished border
design will be symmetrically balanced out from the

centre, and you will have the same number of
unworked threads at each side.

APPLYING A BAND

Use this technique for decorating purchased towels.
Embroider the design on the evenweave band in
exactly the same way as for a prepared towel. Steam
press the embroidery on the wrong side, and then

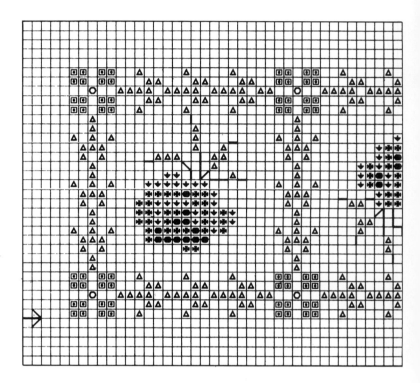

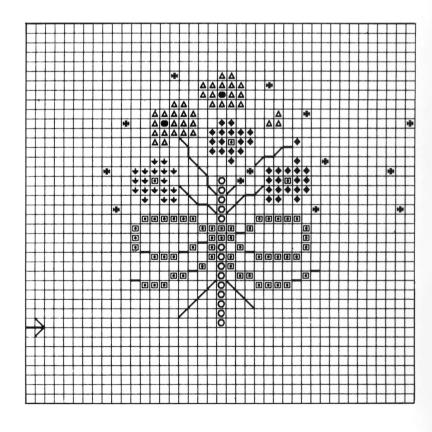

FLORAL BORDER ▶	DMC	ANCHOR	MADEIRA
↓ Yellow	726	295	0109
◆ Orange	741	304	0114
△ Rust	721	324	0308
⊡ Blue	3755	130	1013
● Deep blue	792	941	0905
✸ Mint green	959	186	1113
○ Green	704	256	1308

Note: bks around stems in green.

make 12mm (½in) turnings all around, and baste. Pin and baste the band to the right side of the towel, 6cm (2½in) up from the lower edge. You may wish to insert a narrow lace edging between the band and the towel, to soften the edge. Machine stitch in place, using matching sewing thread. Remove the basting stitches and steam press to finish.

ROSE BORDER ▼	DMC	ANCHOR	MADEIRA
○ Yellow	726	295	0109
↓ Pale pink	818	23	0502
✳ Pink	776	25	0606
• Deep pink	604	51	0504
⊡ Blue	341	117	0901
△ Green	563	215	1209

Centre

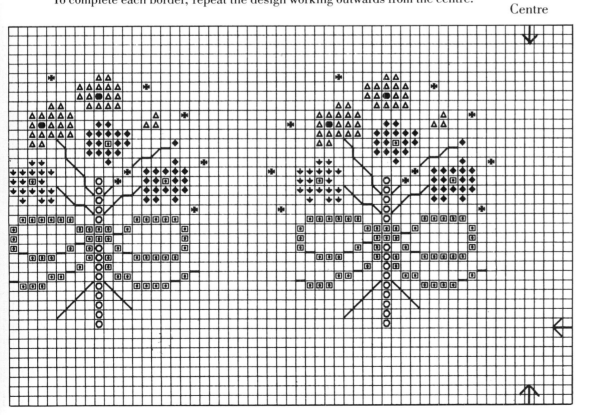

To complete each border, repeat the design working outwards from the centre.

Centre

111

Sachets and Herb Pillow

What could be more delightful than a
sweet-scented sachet to place in a
drawer or wardrobe, or a fragrant herb
pillow to help induce sleep? These
sachets are easy to make and a
pleasure to receive (if you can bear to
part with them).

SACHETS AND HERB PILLOW

YOU WILL NEED

For the Dog Violet pot pourri sack, measuring 9.5cm × 15.5cm (3¾in × 6¼in) approximately:

Two 14.5cm × 21cm (5¾in × 8½in) pieces of beige, 18-count Hardanger fabric
46cm (18in) of lilac ribbon, 12mm (½in) wide
Stranded embroidery cotton in the colours given in the appropriate panel
No26 tapestry needle
Pot pourri of your choice for filling

For the Cornflower sachet, measuring 13cm (5in) square, excluding the lace edging:

18cm (7¼in) square of cream, 18-count Aida fabric
15cm (6in) square of cotton net, for backing
90cm (1yd) of cream lace edging, 18mm (¾in) wide
46cm (18in) of lavender ribbon, for bow and loop
Stranded embroidery cotton in the colours given in the appropriate panel
No26 tapestry needle
Pot pourri of your choice for filling

For the Ragged Robin herb pillow, measuring 21.5cm × 14cm (8½in × 5½in):

Two 27cm × 19.5cm (10¾in × 7¾in) pieces of cream, 18-count Aida fabric
70cm (27in) of cream lace edging, 18mm (¾in) wide
Stranded embroidery cotton in the colours given in the appropriate panel
No26 tapestry needle
Pot pourri of your choice for filling

THE EMBROIDERY

Prepare fabric, marking the centre lines of each design with basting stitches, with the exception of the pot pourri sack. For this, measure up 6cm (2½in) from one short edge and baste a line across from one side to the other. This marks the base line.

Mount the fabric in a hoop or frame, following the instructions on pages 8-9. Referring to the appropriate chart, complete the cross stitching, using two strands of embroidery cotton in the needle for both the cross stitch and the backstitching. For the pot pourri sack, start from the centre of the base line. For the other designs, start from the centre and work out. Embroider the main areas first, and then finish with the backstitching. Steam press on the wrong side.

MAKING THE POT POURRI SACK

Place the two pieces of fabric with right sides together and trim to measure 11.5cm × 18cm (4½in × 7¼in). Taking a 12mm (½in) seam allowance, stitch the side and bottom seams. Roll a narrow hem around the top of the sack, stitching it by hand.

Fold the ribbon in half and, leaving a loop 5cm (2in) long at the folded end, stitch it to the side of the sack, about 3cm (1¼in) down from the top edge. Fill the sack with pot pourri and tie the ribbon securely.

MAKING THE LACE-TRIMMED SACHET

Trim the embroidered fabric to measure 15cm (6in) square. With right sides together, and taking a 12mm (½in) seam allowance, stitch it to the net, leaving an opening of 6.5cm (2½in). Trim across the corners; turn the sachet right side out and press the edges.

Join the short edges of the lace with a small french seam. Gather the lace and stitch it by hand to the edge of the sachet, allowing extra fullness at the corners. Decorate with a bow and loop of ribbon at one corner.

Fill the sachet with pot pourri, and slipstitch the opening.

MAKING THE HERB PILLOW

Trim the two pieces of fabric to measure 24.5cm × 16.5cm (9½in × 6½in). With right sides together, and taking a 12mm (½in) seam allowance, join the two pieces, leaving a gap of 8cm (3½in) in one side. Trim across the corners; turn the pillow right side out, and press the edges. Add the lace, as for the sachet; then fill with pot pourri or lavender, and slipstitch the opening.

DOG VIOLET ►		DMC	ANCHOR	MADEIRA
⊟	Ecru	Ecru	926	Ecru
⊡	Pale mauve	554	97	0711
⊞	Mauve	208	110	0804
▲	Reddish orange	350	11	0213
⊠	Pale green	3364	260	1603
◆	Dark green	3345	268	1406

Note: bks main stems in dark green and leaf rib in pale green.

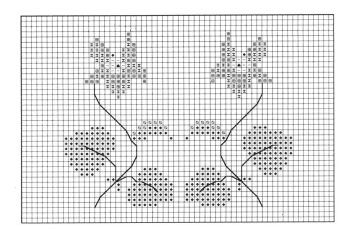

CORNFLOWER ◄		DMC	ANCHOR	MADEIRA
◇	Pale mauve	210	108	0802
⊓	Light navy	336	150	1007
⊠	Blue	340	118	0902
▼	Dark blue	793	121	0906
↓	Green	3347	266	1408
◆	Dark green	3345	268	1406

Note: bks in green.

RAGGED ROBIN ▼		DMC	ANCHOR	MADEIRA
•	Ecru	Ecru	926	Ecru
⊠	Pale pink	3609	85	0710
△	Medium pink	3608	86	0709
⊡	Deep pink	3607	87	0708
⊞	Pale green	3348	264	1409
	Green*	3347	266	1408
▼	Dark green	3345	268	1406
●	Purplish brown	315	896	0810

Note: bks centres of two lower flowers in ecru, and bud stalks in purplish brown, all main stems in green, and centres of five upper flowers in pale green.*

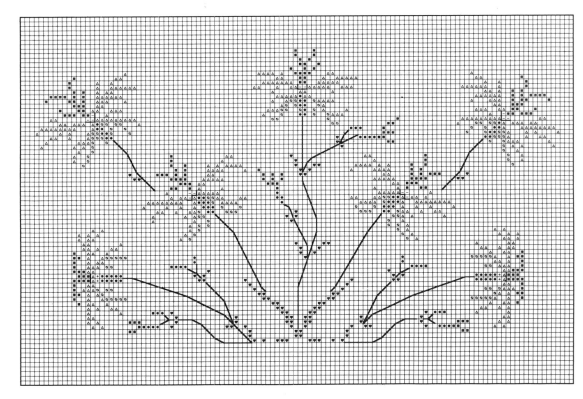

Floral Basket Liner

Embroidered with a simple border of pastel-coloured flowers, this liner, with its pretty scalloped edge, is the perfect accessory for a basket of beautifully-wrapped sweets or petit fours. The edge is bound with a contrasting binding, but you could buttonhole stitch around the edge as an alternative. Embroider the cross stitching first, then the buttonholing; finally, trim the fabric up to the outer twisted edge of the stitching.

FLORAL
BASKET LINER

YOU WILL NEED

For a Basket liner, measuring 30cm × 25cm
(12in × 10in):

*34cm × 29cm (13½in × 11½in) of white,
28-count linen,
Stranded embroidery cotton in the colours
given in the panel
No26 tapestry needle
115cm (1¼yd) of contrast cotton bias binding,
12mm (½in) wide
Sewing thread to match the contrast binding
15cm (6in) square of cardboard for a template
(use a breakfast cereal box, or similar packaging)
Tracing paper*

•

THE EMBROIDERY

Stretch the prepared fabric in a frame and, following the chart, cross stitch the motifs given in one
quarter section, as marked by the basting stitches.
Use two strands of thread in the needle and work
one cross stitch over two threads of fabric throughout. For the remaining three sections, turn the frame
through 90 degrees and repeat the cross stitching.

Remember not to strand the thread across the
back of the fabric, or it will show through on the
right side. Remove the finished embroidery from
the frame, retaining the basting stitches, and steam
press on the wrong side.

DRAWING THE SCALLOPED EDGE

Using a soft pencil, trace the outline of the quarter
section, as shown, and transfer it to the cardboard
(to do this, simply turn the tracing over and,
placing it on the cardboard, pencil over the back
of the outline). Cut out the template.

Lay the embroidery face down and position the
template over one quarter section, matching the
straight lines to the basted lines. Lightly draw

around the scalloped edge with a pencil. Repeat for
the other three quarter sections, cut around the
scalloped edge, and remove the basting stitches.

BINDING THE EDGE

With right sides and raw edges together, pin and
baste the binding around the edge (see page 10),

To complete the
embroidery, turn the
fabric through 90
degrees and repeat
the design
three times.

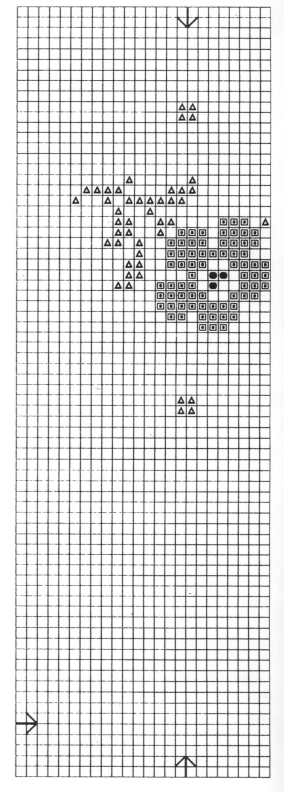

beginning in the corner of one scallop. Where the two ends of the binding meet, overlap by 2cm (¾in), turning the raw, overlapped end under by 6mm (¼in) to neaten it. Using matching sewing thread, machine stitch or backstitch in place.

Turn the binding over the edge of the fabric, and hem, sewing into the back of the first stitching to prevent the thread from showing through.

FLORAL BASKET LINER ▼	DMC	ANCHOR	MADEIRA
✚ Yellow	725	306	0108
✱ Pink	961	40	0610
• Dark red	326	20	0407
⊡ Blue	341	117	0901
△ Olive green	733	280	1611

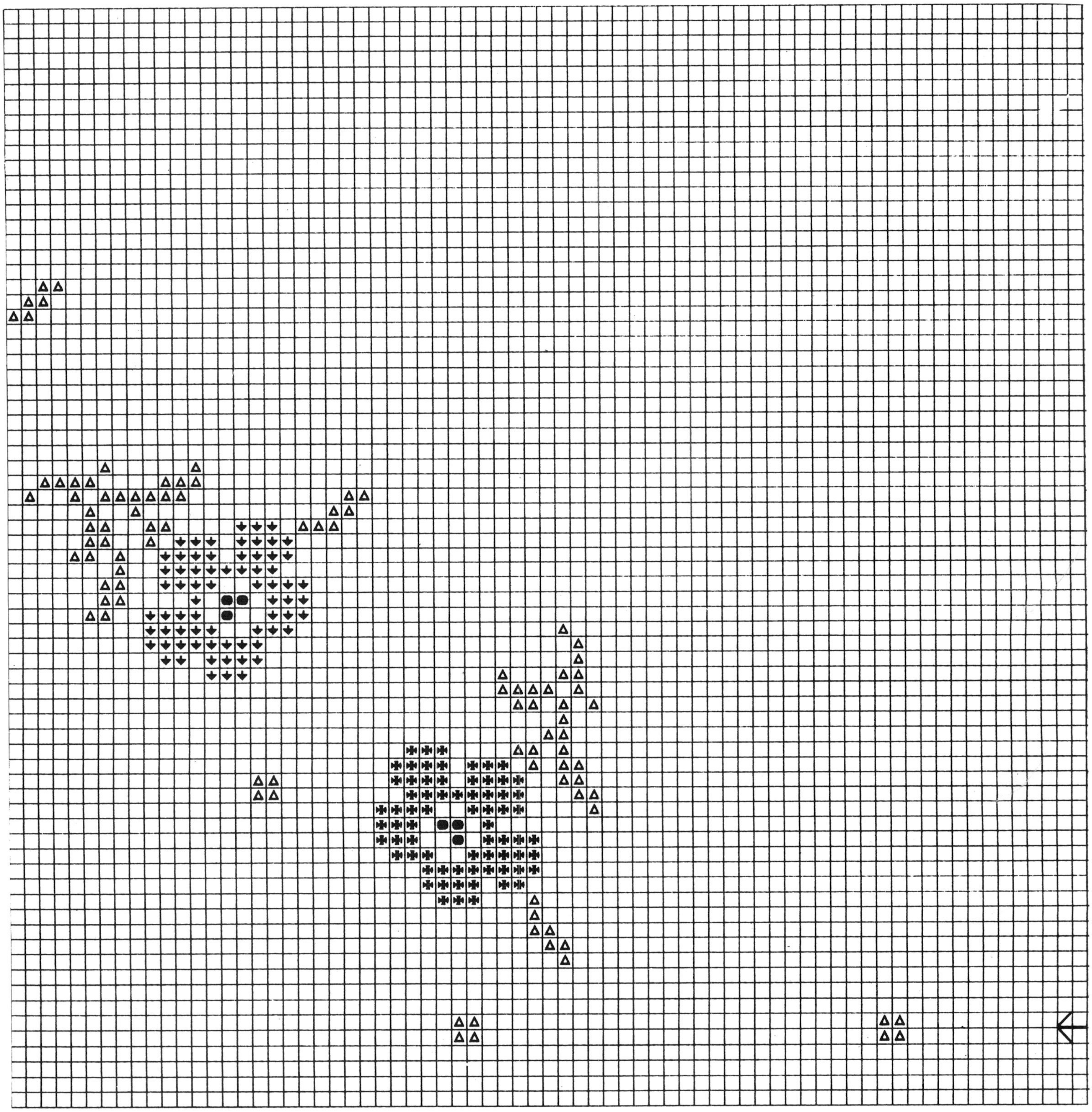

Framed Bramble and Eglantine

The bramble is a member of the rose family, its white or pale pink flowers of early summer giving way to a profusion of berries in autumn. The eglantine, or briar rose, is a fragrant wild hedgerow rose, much pinker than the common dog rose.

FRAMED BRAMBLE AND EGLANTINE

YOU WILL NEED

For each picture, set in a frame with a picture area measuring 18cm × 12.5cm (7in × 5in):

27cm × 23cm (10¾in × 9in) of eau-de-Nil, 18-count Aida fabric
Stranded embroidery cotton in the colours given in the panel
No26 tapestry needle
Strong thread, for lacing across the back
Cross-over frame (for suppliers, see page 160)

●

THE EMBROIDERY

For each picture, prepare the fabric, marking the centre lines of the design with basting stitches, and set it in a frame (see page 9). Embroider from the centre of the design, completing the main areas first, and then the backstitching. Use two strands of thread throughout, except for fine details, such as the stamens, where one thread is recommended. Gently steam press the finished embroidery on the wrong side. Retain the central basting stitches at this stage.

ASSEMBLING THE PICTURES

Each picture is assembled in the same way. Trim the edges of the embroidery until it measures 23cm × 18cm (9in × 7¼in). Mark the central horizontal and vertical lines on the mount provided and, matching these with the central basting stitches, lace the embroidery over the mount, following the instructions on page 10. Remove basting stitches. Assemble according to the manufacturer's instructions.

EGLANTINE ◀		DMC	ANCHOR	MADEIRA
↳	White	White	2	White
·	Cream	712	926	2101
Ϋ	Palest pink	3689	49	0607
I	Pale pink	605	60	0613
⋰	Pink	604	66	0614
+	Deep pink	603	62	0701
⊣	Lemon	744	301	0112
⌐	Yellow	743	297	0113
↲	Bright yellow	972	298	0107
x	Orange	970	316	0204
11	Deep orange	900	333	0208
:-	Green	3347	266	1408
⊥	Medium green	3346	262	1407
T	Dark green	3345	268	1406
—	Yellowish green	472	264	1414
	Dark yellowish green*	470	267	1503
⅃	Fawn	729	890	2209
⊐	Yellowish brown	831	889	2201

Note: bks rosehips in dark yellowish green, stamens in yellow, pollen tips on stamens, adjacent flower centre and dying leaf in yellowish brown, leaf stalks in dark green, and rosehip stalks in medium green.*

BRAMBLE ▼		DMC	ANCHOR	MADEIRA
·	White	White	2	White
/	Soft pink	819	271	0501
↳	Pink	3688	66	0605
T	Deep pink	3350	42	0603
—	Pale mauve	3609	85	0710
x	Purplish pink	3608	86	0709
⊐	Navy	939	152	1009
:-	Pale green	3013	842	1605
I	Green	3363	262	1602
+	Dark green	520	862	1514
⅃	Yellowish green	3348	264	1409
⋰	Greyish green	3052	859	1509
⊣	Ginger brown	433	371	2008
⊔	Dark brown	3031	905	2003
⊥	Dark grey	413	401	1713
■	Black	310	403	Black

Note: bks base of new fruit in ginger brown, tips of stamens and base of flowers in dark green, stamens in pale green and all stems in yellowish green.

Lacy Gifts

A peach rose on the pincushion is edged with a delicate cream border, echoed by broderie anglaise. The bag, filled with lavender from your garden, will remind you of summer throughout the rest of the year. To complete the trio, there is a bookmark with a lacy trim.

LACY GIFTS

YOU WILL NEED

For the Pincushion, measuring 17.5cm
(7in) square, excluding the lace:

25cm (10in) square of cream, 14-count Aida fabric
20cm (8in) square of cream backing fabric
1.6m (1¾yds) of cream broderie anglaise,
5cm (2in) wide
4 pale peach ribbon roses
Stranded embroidery cotton in the colours given
in the panel
No24 tapestry needle
Polyester filling

For the Lavender bag, measuring 12.5cm × 17cm
(5in × 6¾in):

20cm × 22cm (8in × 8½in) of cream,
14-count Aida fabric
15cm × 17cm (6in × 6½in) of cream backing
fabric
35cm (14in) of cream broderie anglaise, 5cm
(2in) wide
50cm (20in) of peach satin ribbon, 6mm (¼in)
wide
Stranded embroidery cotton in the colours given
in the panel
No24 tapestry needle

For the Bookmark, measuring 9cm × 20.5cm
(3½in × 8in):

Stranded embroidery cotton in the colours given
in the panel
No24 tapestry needle
Prepared bookmark, in ivory (for suppliers, see
page 160)

•

THE EMBROIDERY

Stretch the fabric for the pincushion or the lavender bag in a hoop or frame, as explained on page 8. The bookmark may be held in the hand when working the embroidery.

Following the correct chart, start the embroidery at the centre of the design, using two strands of embroidery cotton in the needle for the pincushion or lavender bag and one strand for the bookmark. Work each stitch over one block of fabric in each

direction. Make sure that all the top crosses run in the same direction and that each row is worked into the same holes as the top or bottom of the row before, so that you do not leave a space between rows. Lightly steam press the finished embroidery.

MAKING THE PINCUSHION

Trim the embroidery to measure 20cm (8in) square. Using a tiny french seam, join the short edges of the broderie anglaise together, then run a gathering thread close to the straight edge of the lace. Pulling up the gathers to fit, lay the lace on the right side of the embroidery, with the decorative edge facing inward and the straight edge parallel to the edge of the fabric and just inside the 12mm (½in) seam allowance. Baste in position, adjusting the gathers to allow extra fullness at the corners. Machine in place.

With right sides together, pin and machine the backing fabric and the embroidered piece together, enclosing the broderie anglaise edging and leaving a gap of 5cm (2in) at one side. Trim across the corners; turn the pincushion right side out, and insert the polyester filling. Slipstitch the opening to close it.

Lavender bag ▼

MAKING THE LAVENDER BAG

Trim the embroidered fabric to measure 15cm × 17cm (6in × 6½in). With right sides together, baste and machine stitch the embroidery to the backing fabric, stitching down the sides and across the bottom and taking a 12mm (½in) seam allowance.

Turn to the right side. Turn a single 12mm (½in) hem around the top. Join the short edges of the broderie anglaise with a tiny french seam, then run a gathering thread close to the straight edge of the lace. Pulling up the gathers to fit and with the right side of the lace to the wrong side of the bag, baste and then machine stitch the broderie anglaise in place around the top of the bag. Gently steam press.

Fill the bag with lavender and tie with a ribbon, placing it around the space between the two areas of embroidery.

BOOKMARK, LAVENDER BAG AND PINCUSHION ▼		DMC	ANCHOR	MADEIRA
◨	Cream	746	275	0101
⊥	Light peach	353	6	0304
⊠	Dark peach	352	9	0303
▽	Light green	3348	264	1409
▬	Medium green	3052	844	1509
■	Dark green*	936	263	1507

Dark green used for bks outline of roses on pincushion only.

Bookmark ▼

Pincushion ▼

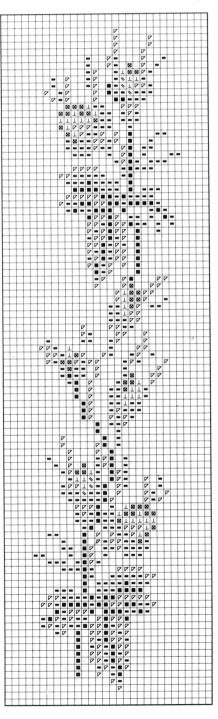

DECORATIVE TOUCHES FOR THE HOME

It is the small personal touches that turn a house into a home, and hand-embroidered cushions and table linen are an ideal way of adding elegance to your surroundings.
The foxglove cushion and bellpull — a challenge for cross stitch enthusiasts — would look at home in almost any room of the house.
The table linen includes a choice of tablemats with either a silverweed border or one of pansies and roses, as well as a scalloped design with fruits and berries.

Baskets and Wreaths

A profusion of white lace and flowers gives a light and airy feel to these cushions. The bright shades of the roses are complemented by the gentler blue and mauve flowers, making this trio a delightful addition to any home.

BASKETS AND WREATHS

YOU WILL NEED

For each cushion, measuring 40cm (16in) square:

21.5cm (8½in) square of white, 14-count
Aida fabric
Stranded embroidery cotton in the colours given
in the panel
No24 tapestry needle
42cm (16½in) square of lace fabric
Two 42cm (16½in) squares of white backing fabric
85cm (34in) of gathered lace edging, 5cm (2in)
wide, for the edge of the embroidered panel
1.8m (2yds) of gathered lace edging, 4cm (1½in)
wide, for the edge of the cushion
42.5cm (17in) square cushion pad

NOTE If you are making the easy care cover, you
will require, in place of the two squares of backing
fabric, one 42cm (16½in) square and two more
pieces, both 42cm (16½in) long, one 23cm (9in)
wide, and one 33cm (13in) wide

•

THE EMBROIDERY

Prepare the fabric and stretch it in a frame as explained on page 9. Following the chart, start the embroidery at the centre of the design, using two strands of embroidery cotton in the needle. Work each stitch over a block of fabric in each direction, making sure that all the top crosses run in the same direction and each row is worked into the same holes as the top or bottom of the row before, so that you do not leave a space between the rows.

MAKING UP

Each cover is made up in the same way. Gently steam press the embroidered fabric on the wrong side, then turn under 12mm (½in) on all sides, mitring the corners as explained on page 10. Baste the wider of the lace edgings around the embroidered fabric, positioning it just under the turned edge and joining the ends of the lace together with a narrow french seam.

Centre the panel over the lace fabric. Pin it in position and then appliqué the panel to the lace by slipstitching around the edge through all layers. Take the remaining lace edging and, again joining the ends with a narrow french seam, pin and baste it

around the edge of the lace fabric. The decorative edge should face inward and the straight edge of the lace should lie parallel to the edge of the fabric and just inside the 12mm (½in) seam allowance.

Take one of the pieces of backing fabric and lay the prepared lace fabric over it, still with the frill lying flat on the lace, facing inward. With the wrong side of the lace fabric to the right side of the backing, pin, baste and stitch through all three layers, stitching through the straight edge of the lace, just within the 12mm (½in) seam allowance.

With right sides together, join the remaining piece of backing fabric to the cushion front, leaving a 25cm (10in) gap at one side. Turn the cover right side out; insert the cushion pad, and slipstitch to close.

EASY CARE VERSION

If you prefer a cover that can quickly be slipped off and on, for ease of laundering, you can make one with an overlap across the centre back.

Make up the front of the cover as described above. Take the wider of the two pieces of backing fabric; neaten one of the long edges and then press and stitch a 12mm (½in) hem. Take the other piece, and again on a long edge turn under 6mm (¼in) and then a further 12mm (½in) and hem. Lay the shorter piece over the longer one, overlapping the prepared edges, to make a 42cm (16½in) square; baste and stitch the sides.

Place the prepared back and cushion front with right sides together and, taking a 12mm (½in) seam, stitch all around the edge. Turn the cover right side out and insert the cushion pad through the opening across the back.

BASKETS AND WREATHS ▶		DMC	ANCHOR	MADEIRA
‹	Light pink	776	73	0606
+	Medium pink	894	26	0408
o	Dark pink	892	28	0413
@	Mauve	208	111	0804
v	Yellow	745	292	0112
%	Light blue	932	920	1602
−	Dark blue	930	922	1005
s	Light green	369	213	1309
=	Medium green	368	214	1310
‡	Dark green	367	216	1312
x	Light brown	950	882	2309
›	Dark brown	407	914	2312

Note: the same combination is used for the Baskets design and the Wreaths design, on pages 136-7.

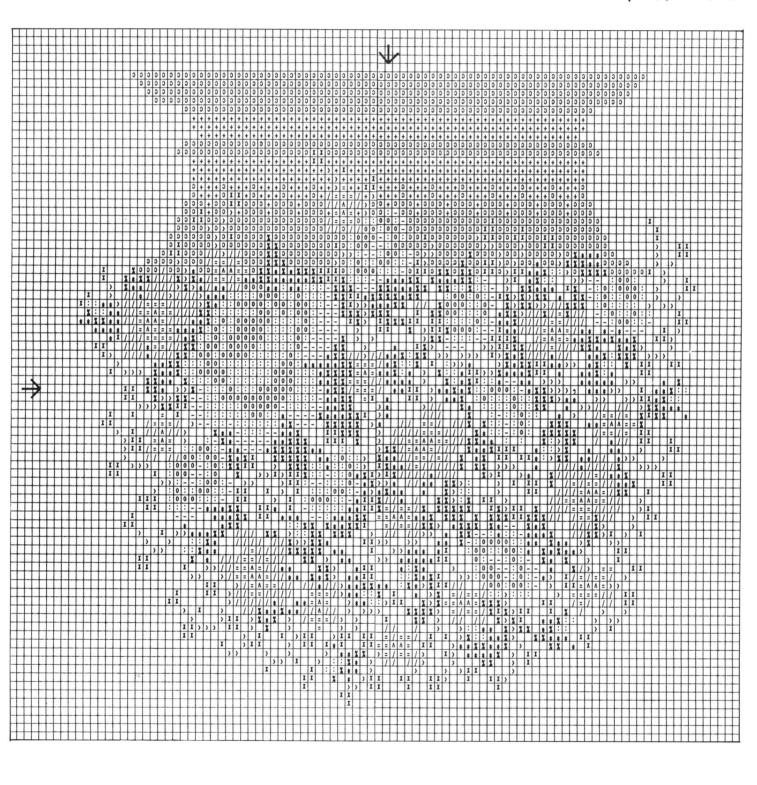

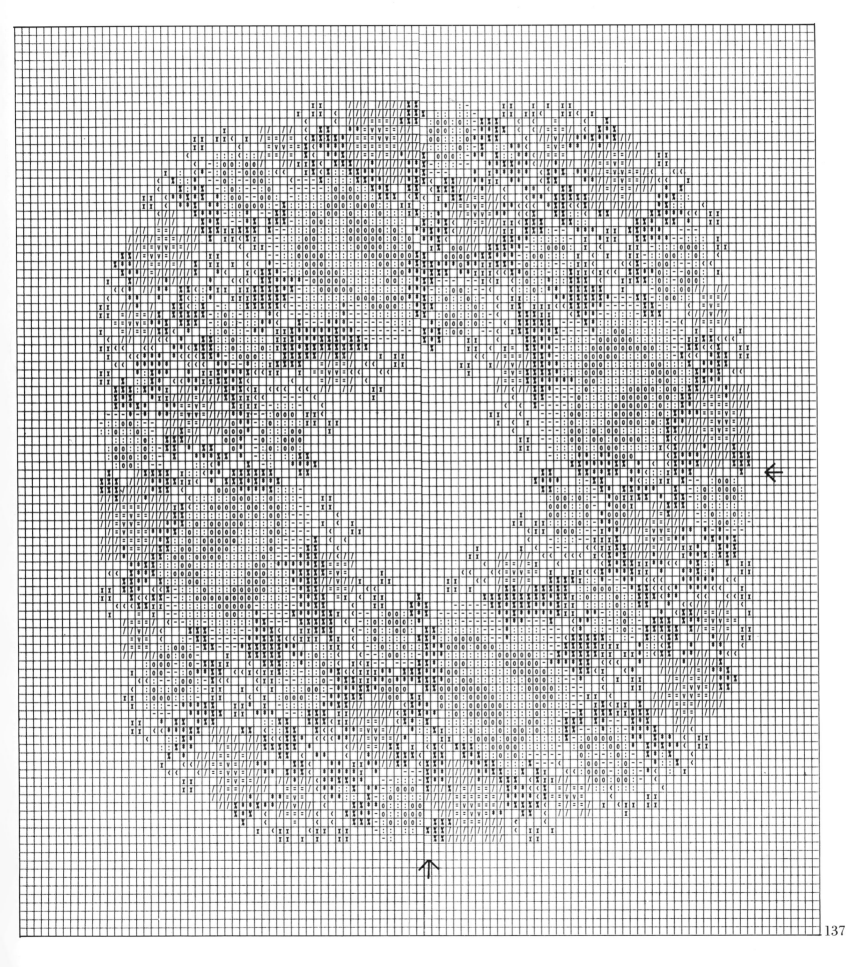

Foxglove Duo

This beautiful cushion would enhance any sitting room, and to add that extra dimension, why not complement it with an elegant wall hanger?

FOXGLOVE DUO

YOU WILL NEED

For the Foxglove cushion cover, measuring
47cm (18½in) square:

*52cm (21in) of cream, 14-count Aida fabric
48.5cm (19½in) square of furnishing fabric, for
the cushion back
Two 48.5cm (19½in) squares of strong unbleached
cotton fabric, for the inner cover
Stranded embroidery cotton in the colours given
in the panel
No24 tapestry needle
3m (3½yds) of matching green (or deep pink)
cushion cord, 6mm (¼in) in diameter
47cm (18½in) cushion pad*

For the Wall hanging, measuring 41cm × 16.5cm
(16½in × 6½in):

*50cm × 25cm (20in × 10in) of cream, 18-count
Aida fabric
46cm × 20.5cm (18in × 8in) of cream
lining fabric
40.5cm × 16cm (16in × 6¼in) of
iron-on interfacing
Stranded embroidery cotton in the colours given
in the panel
No26 tapestry needle
Pair of wooden hangers (for suppliers, see page 160)*

•

THE EMBROIDERY

Prepare the fabric for your chosen design, marking the centre lines with basting stitches, and mount it in a frame (see page 9). In both cases, start to embroider from the centre of the design. For the cushion, use three strands of cotton in the needle for both the cross stitch and the backstitch.

The wall hanging is adapted from the cushion design, as seen in the picture. The stalk of the Timothy grass on the left-hand side is lowered so that it extends only over 32 threads from the upper leaf to the head: this is to balance the effect. Use two strands of thread in the needle for cross stitching and backstitching the grass stalks, and one thread for backstitching the finer details.

When you have finished your chosen design, gently steam press on the wrong side.

MAKING THE CUSHION COVER

With right sides together, and taking a 12mm (½in) seam, join the two pieces of strong cotton for the inner lining, leaving a 25cm (10in) opening at one side. Trim across the corners and turn the lining inside out. Insert the cushion pad and slipstitch the opening.

Trim the embroidered fabric to measure 48.5cm (19½in) square, keeping the design centred. Remove the central basting lines and, with right sides together, join the embroidered fabric and the cover backing fabric, again leaving a 25cm (10in) opening. Repeat the same process as for the inner lining.

To complete the cover, trim the edges with cord, forming it into loops at the corners and slipstitching it in place.

THE WALL HANGING

Centre the interfacing on the back of the embroidery and pin it in place. Remove the basting stitches and iron the interfacing in position. Trim the long edges of the embroidery until it measures 19cm (7½in) wide. Turn in the long edges by 12mm (½in) and press.

On the two short edges, make a 6mm (¼in) turning. Make a second turning, 4cm (1½in) deep, taking the fabric over a rod at the top and bottom. Baste and neatly hem in place.

Turn in the long edges of the lining fabric by 12mm (½in) and turn in the short edges so that the piece will neatly cover all raw edges and hems at the back of the work. Slipstitch in place.

FOXGLOVE CUSHION ▶		DMC	ANCHOR	MADEIRA
·	Cream	746	275	0101
I	Rose pink	3609	85	0710
∴	Medium rose	3608	86	0709
T	Deep rose	3607	87	0708
X	Dull pink	223	894	0812
⊥	Dusky pink	778	968	0808
U	Purplish red	315	896	0810
⊣	Lime green	472	264	1414
⊰	Bluish green	320	216	1311
	Pale green*	522	859	1513
—	Green	3348	264	1409
Y	Medium green	3347	262	1408
+	Dark green	3346	817	1407
⊐	Very dark green	3345	268	1406
ʔ	Light fawn	3047	886	2205
⊢	Fawn	612	832	2108

Note: bks foxglove bells in purplish red, Timothy grass stalks and leaf in bluish green and seeds in lime green, bent grass stalk in pale green*, ground elder flower stalks in dark green, red campion stalks and flower in green, and style of dead foxglove flower in deep rose; for the wallhanger, you will not need dull pink, dusky pink, fawn, light fawn, pale green, very dark green, and green.

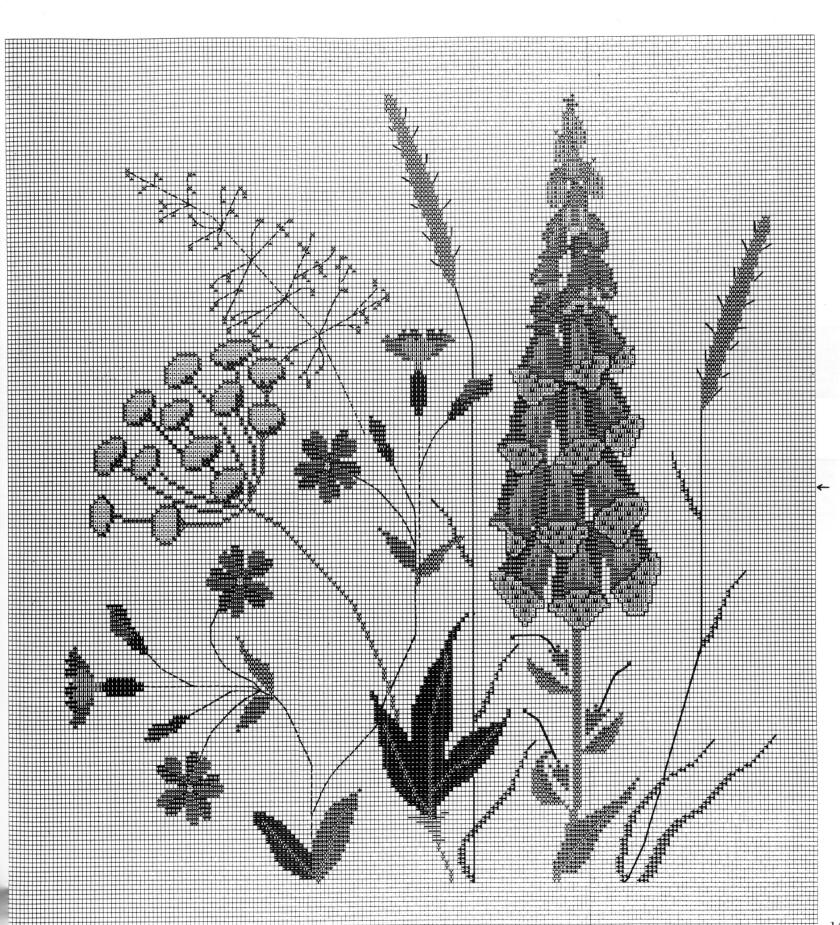

Rose Corner

Romance is certainly in the air with
this beautiful tablecloth, embroidered
with a ring of red roses and
accompanied by a matching crystal
bowl and silver-framed picture.
This set will brighten up a corner of
the darkest room, and if the bowl is
filled with pot pourri this will provide
a lingering fragrance of summer
to complete the effect.

ROSE CORNER

YOU WILL NEED

*For the tablecloth, measuring approximately
1m (39in) square:*

*90cm (36in) square of white, 25-count
Lugana fabric
Stranded embroidery cotton in the colours given
in the panel
3m (3½yds) of gathered lace, 9cm (3½in) wide
No24 tapestry needle*

*For the bowl lid, with an inset measuring 9cm
(3½in) in diameter:*

*14cm (5½in) square of white, 14-count
Aida fabric
Stranded embroidery cotton in the colours given
in the panel
No24 tapestry needle
Crystal bowl with prepared lid (for suppliers, see
page 160)*

*For the picture, in an oval frame measuring
8cm × 10cm (3in × 4in):*

*13cm × 15cm (5in × 6in) of white, 14-count
Aida fabric
Stranded embroidery cotton in the colours given
in the panel
No24 tapestry needle
Oval frame (for suppliers, see page 160)*

•

THE TABLECLOTH

Prepare the linen and stretch it in a hoop, as
explained on page 8. Alternatively, as the evenweave linen is a firmly-woven fabric, it is possible
to embroider without a hoop. Following the chart,
begin with the central circle, then work outward.
Use two strands of embroidery cotton in the needle
throughout, and work each stitch over two threads
of fabric in each direction.

MAKING UP

Steam press on the wrong side. Make a hem 12mm
(½in) deep around the outside of the cloth, mitring
the corners (see page 10). Next, measure 24cm
(9½in) in each side from each corner and lightly
mark the right side of the cloth with a soft pencil,
12mm (½in) in from the edge.

Pin and baste the gathered lace to the tablecloth,
positioning the straight edge of the lace 12mm
(½in) in from the edge. When you reach the pencil
marks, baste the lace across the corner of the cloth,
between the two marks. Slipstitch the lace in place.

BOWL LID AND PICTURE

For each, prepare the fabric, basting the central
vertical and horizontal lines, and set it in a hoop, as
explained on page 8. Use two strands of embroidery
cotton in the needle and work over one block of
fabric in each direction. Start at the centre and
work outward. Steam press the finished work and
mount it as explained in the manufacturer's
instructions.

Picture ▶

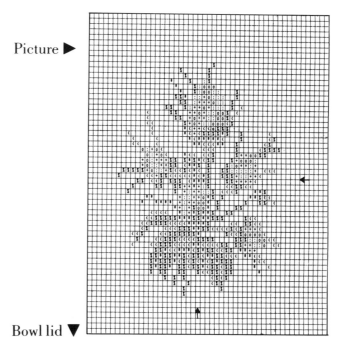

Bowl lid ▼

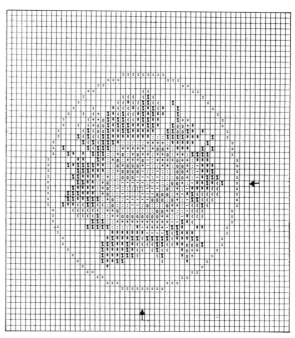

▲
Tablecloth

RED ROSE TABLECLOTH, BOWL AND PICTURE		DMC	ANCHOR	MADEIRA			DMC	ANCHOR	MADEIRA
−	Pink	892	28	0413	⟨ Light green	369	213	1309
:	Light red	666	46	0210	% Medium green	368	214	1310
+	Medium red	304	42	0511	✦ Dark green	367	216	1312
o	Dark red	814	44	0514	= Grey	415	398	1803

Note: One skein of each colour is sufficient for all three designs.

Silverweed Table Set

Potentilla anserina (silverweed) is used for an elegant design for a place setting for one. A complete set would make the perfect gift for a golden wedding anniversary. Silverweed is an attractive yellow-flowered roadside plant, with leaves that are a delicate silvery green on the underside. It flowers in the summer months, thriving in dampish conditions.

SILVERWEED TABLE SET

YOU WILL NEED

For one placemat, measuring 46cm × 34cm
(18½in × 13½in):

*50cm × 39cm (20in × 15½in) of cream,
28-count evenweave fabric
Stranded embroidery cotton in the colours given
in the panel
No26 tapestry needle*

For one napkin, measuring 37cm (14½) square:

*42cm (16½in) of cream, 28-count evenweave
fabric
Stranded embroidery cotton in the colours given
in the panel
No26 tapestry needle*

*Alternatively, ready-prepared placemats and
napkins can be obtained from specialist
suppliers (see page 160)*

●

THE EMBROIDERY

For either the placemat or the napkin, begin by
preparing the edges of the fabric in the usual way
(see page 8).

For the placemat, mark the central horizontal
line across the fabric with a line of basting stitches.
From the left-hand side of the fabric, measure in
along this line for 10cm (4in). A vertical line at this
point marks the start of the embroidery. Set the
fabric in a frame (see page 9), and work out from
the central point to complete two motifs, one on
either side of the horizontal line.

For the napkin, which features only one motif,
baste a vertical line 10cm (4in) in from the left-
hand side and a horizontal one 13.5cm (5¼in) up
from the lower edge. The centre point of the motif
is the point where these two lines intersect.

For both the placemat and the napkin, use three
strands of embroidery cotton in the needle for the
cross stitch and the backstitching, working over two
fabric threads. Gently steam press the finished
embroideries on the wrong side.

FRINGING

Trim 2.5cm (1in) all around the finished embroideries, so that the placemat measures 46cm × 34cm
(18½in × 13½in) and the napkin measures 37cm
(14½in) square.

On all four sides of each, withdraw a single fabric
thread 12mm (½in) in from the outer edge.

The fringing can be secured in one of several
ways: by machining around the rectangle (placemat)
or square (napkin) left by the withdrawn threads,
using either straight stitch or a narrow zigzag stitch;
by overcasting every alternate thread by hand, or by
hemstitching, as shown below.

When you have secured the line by your chosen
method, remove all cross threads below the stitched
line to complete the fringe.

HEMSTITCH

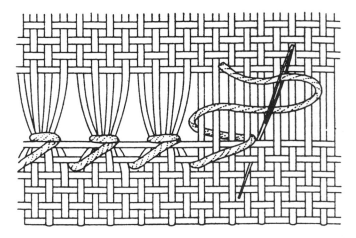

If you prefer to secure your fringing by hemstitch,
remove a single thread from the fabric at the hem-
line (the start of the fringe). Bring the needle out on
the right side, two threads below the drawn-thread
line. Working from left to right, pick up either two or
three threads, as shown in the diagram. Bring the
needle out again and insert it behind the fabric, to
emerge two threads down, ready to make the next
stitch. Before reinserting the needle, pull the thread
tight, so that the bound threads form a neat group. To
complete the fringe, remove the weft threads below
the hemstitching.

SILVERWEED ◀		DMC	ANCHOR	MADEIRA
·	Yellow	727	293	0110
—	Deep yellow	726	295	0109
x	Gold	725	306	0113
Ϯ	Silver green	368	240	1310
∴	Light green	3347	266	1408
+	Green	3346	817	1407
Ц	Ginger brown	782	308	2212

Note: bks flower stems, outlines and centres in ginger brown, and leaf stalks in light green.

Four Seasons Placemat

This delightful placemat, with its four seasons design, featuring cherries, strawberries, rosehips and cranberries, has a prettily scalloped border, edged with contrast cotton binding.
A single placemat makes a cheerful accessory when eating alone, or it could double as a traycloth. You could also make one for each member of the family, perhaps embroidering just a single motif on each one, placing it at the centre top, to reduce the amount of embroidery involved.

FOUR SEASONS PLACEMAT

YOU WILL NEED

For a Placemat measuring 39cm × 29cm
(15½in × 11½in):

*46cm × 35cm (18in × 14in) of white,
26-count linen
130cm (1½yd) of contrast cotton bias binding,
2.5cm (1in) wide
Stranded embroidery cotton in the colours
given in the panel
No26 tapestry needle
Sewing thread to match the contrast binding
20cm × 15cm (8in × 6in) of cardboard for a
template (use a breakfast cereal box or
similar packaging)
Tracing paper*

•

THE EMBROIDERY

Prepare the edges of the fabric and baste the centre both ways. Then, following the measurements given on the chart, baste the central rectangle, which forms the positioning lines for each motif. The completed rectangle should measure 200 threads across by 140 threads down.

With the fabric stretched in a hoop and following the chart and colour keys, complete the embroidery. Use two strands of thread in the needle, and work one cross stitch over two threads throughout.

Steam press on the wrong side. Retain the basting stitches at this stage.

DRAWING THE SCALLOPED EDGE

Using a soft pencil, trace the quarter section of the placemat, as shown on this page. Turn the tracing over; place it on the cardboard, and go over the outline to transfer it to the cardboard. Make sure that the two straight sides meet at an exact right angle. Cut out the template.

Lay the embroidery face down, and place the template over one quarter, matching the straight edges to the central basting stitches. Lightly draw around the scalloped edge. Repeat this for the remaining sections. Carefully cut out the placemat and remove the basting stitches.

BINDING THE EDGE

With right sides and raw edges together, pin and baste the binding around the edge (see page 10), beginning in the corner of one scallop. Where the two ends of the binding meet, overlap by 2cm (¾in), turning the raw, overlapped end under by 6mm (¼in) to neaten it. Using matching sewing thread, machine stitch or backstitch in place.

Bring the binding over the raw edge of the fabric and hem, gently easing it around curves and sewing into the back of the first stitching line to prevent the thread from showing on the right side.

To complete the scalloped outline, reverse the template on the centre lines of each quarter section and draw around.

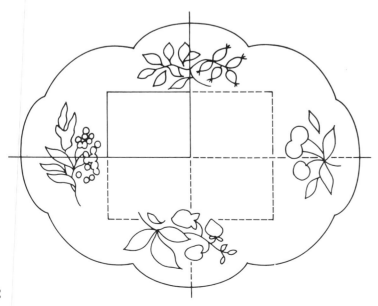

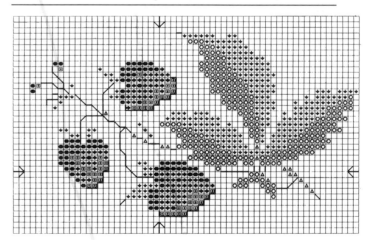

ROSE HIPS ▲		DMC	ANCHOR	MADEIRA
O	Yellow	676	891	2208
•	Red	350	11	0213
△	Rust	976	309	2302
⊡	Blue	3766	167	1109
✱	Sap green	581	267	1609
↓	Browny green	3012	843	1606

Note: use browny green for the tips of the rose hips.

To complete the scalloped outline, reverse the template on the centre lines of each quarter section and draw around.

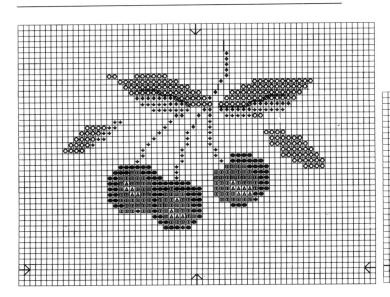

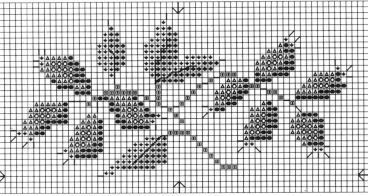

Pansies and Roses

This delightful placemat and napkin
will certainly enhance any table
setting, whether for a candlelit dinner
or a summer party. You might vary the
shades of the roses and pansies to
match either your table setting, or
perhaps the flowers from your own
garden. If you want to change the
design to make up an alternative set,
you could quite easily adapt the motif
to fit a corner instead of running
down the side.

PANSIES AND ROSES

YOU WILL NEED

For one placemat, measuring 33cm × 47cm
(13in × 19in), and one napkin, measuring
40cm (16in) square:

*Ready-prepared, 26-count placemat and napkin
(for suppliers, see page 160)
Stranded embroidery cotton in the colours given
in the panel
No24 tapestry needle*

*NOTE If you prefer not to use ready-prepared table
linen, buy fabric with the same thread count. Work
the embroidery first; trim to the correct size
(including fringe), and withdraw a thread 12mm
(½in) in from each edge. Neatly overcast every
alternate thread, and then remove all cross threads
below the stitched line to complete the fringe.*

PREPARING THE FABRIC

First mark the centre (horizontal) line along
the length of the placemat with a line of basting
stitches. Measure in 2.5cm (1in) from the start of
the fringe on the right-hand side and make a vertical line of basting stitches. Position the centre of
the motif on the horizontal line of basting stitches
and the right-hand edge of the motif along the
vertical line of basting stitches. For the napkin,
measure in and baste lines 12mm (½in) in from the
edge, at one corner, as base lines for positioning.

Stretch the placemat or napkin in a frame (see
page 8).

THE EMBROIDERY

Start at the centre of the appropriate motif and,
using two strands of embroidery cotton in the needle,
work each stitch over two threads of fabric in each
direction. Make sure that all the top crosses run in
the same direction and that each row is worked into
the same holes as the top or bottom of the preceding
row, so that you do not leave a space between rows.

Gently steam press the finished work on the wrong
side to remove all creases.

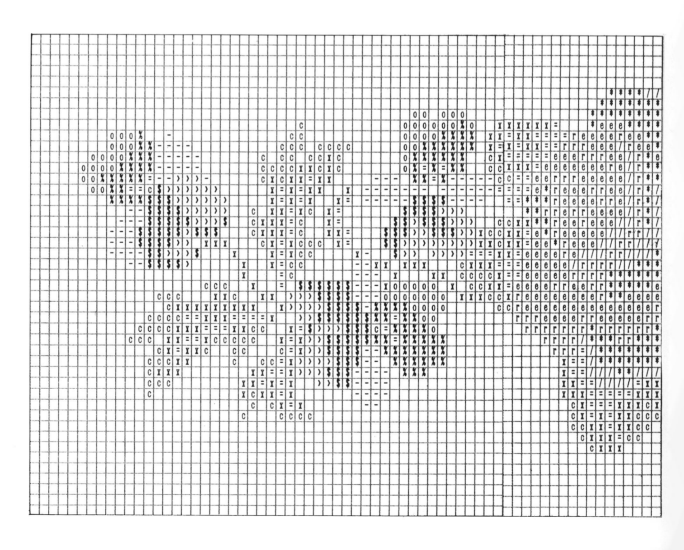

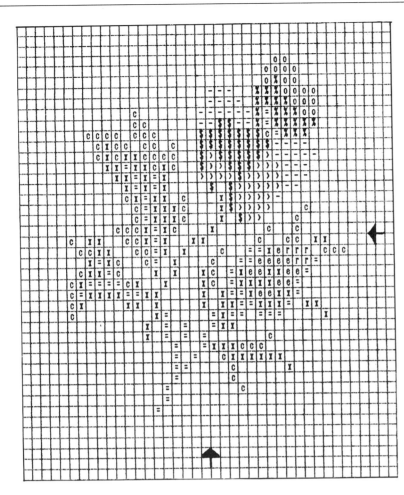

PANSIES AND ROSES		DMC	ANCHOR	MADEIRA
♯	Light pink	3609	85	0710
/	Medium pink	3608	86	0709
r	Dark pink	718	88	0707
e	Darkest pink	915	89	0705
–	Light mauve	210	108	0803
>	Medium mauve	208	111	0804
$	Dark mauve	562	210	1202
%	Light yellow	3078	292	0102
o	Dark yellow	743	301	0113
c	Light green	3052	844	1509
x	Medium green	3347	266	1408
=	Dark green	3051	845	1508

INDEX

ACKNOWLEDGEMENTS

The authors would like to thank the following people for their help with the projects in this book:

Gisela Banbury, Clarice Blakey, Helen Burke, Caroline Davies, Christina Eustace, Lyn Freeman, Janet Grey, Elizabeth Hall, Betty Haste, Cilla King, Kate Riley, Diane Teal, Jenny Thorpe, Violet Watts and Anne Whitbourn.

Thanks are also due to DMC Creative World Ltd, for supplying fabrics and threads, and in some cases the charts, and to Framecraft Miniatures Ltd for supplying some of the frames used in this book, and the box on page 142.

SUPPLIERS

The following mail order company has supplied some of the basic items needed for making up the projects in this book:

Framecraft Miniatures Limited
372/376 Summer Lane
Hockley
Birmingham, B19 3QA
England
Telephone (021) 212 0551

Addresses for Framecraft stockists worldwide
Ireland Needlecraft Pty. Ltd.
2-4 Keppel Drive
Hallam, Victoria 3803
Australia

Danish Art Needlework
PO Box 442, Lethbridge
Alberta T1J 3Z1
Canada

Sanyei Imports
PO Box 5, Hashima Shi
Gifu 501-62
Japan

The Embroidery Shop
286 Queen Street
Masterton
New Zealand

Anne Brinkley Designs Inc.
246 Walnut Street
Newton
Mass. 02160
USA

S A Threads and Cottons Ltd.
43 Somerset Road
Cape Town
South Africa

For information on your nearest stockist of embroidery cotton, contact the following:

DMC

UK
DMC Creative World Limited
62 Pullman Road
Wigston
Leicester, LE8 2DY
Telephone: 0533 811040

USA
The DMC Corporation
Port Kearney Bld.
10 South Kearney
N.J. 07032-0650
Telephone: 201 589 0606

AUSTRALIA
DMC Needlecraft Pty
P.O. Box 317
Earlswood 2206
NSW 2204
Telephone: 02599 3088

COATS AND ANCHOR

UK
Kilncraigs Mill
Alloa
Clackmannanshire
Scotland, FK10 1EG
Telephone: 0259 723431

USA
Coats & Clark
P.O. Box 27067
Dept CO1
Greenville
SC 29616
Telephone: 803 234 0103

AUSTRALIA
Coats Patons Crafts
Thistle Street
Launceston
Tasmania 7250
Telephone: 00344 4222

MADEIRA

UK
Madeira Threads (UK) Limited
Thirsk Industrial Park
York Road, Thirsk
N. Yorkshire, YO7 3BX
Telephone: 0845 524880

USA
Madeira Marketing Limited
600 East 9th Street
Michigan City
IN 46360
Telephone: 219 873 1000

AUSTRALIA
Penguin Threads Pty Limited
25-27 Izett Street
Prahran
Victoria 3181
Telephone: 03529 4400